MASTERING GRAMMAR

Mastering Grammar

A Comprehensive Guide for TESOL Teachers

AMIR ABBAS RAVAEI

Success Publications Sar

Contents

Mastering Grammar: A Comprehensive Guide for TESOL Teachers — 1

About the Book — 2

About the Author — 3

Acknowledgement — 4

1   Introduction — 5

1-1
THE IMPORTANCE OF GRAMMAR IN TESOL

1-2
UNDERSTANDING THE TARGET AUDIENCE

2   TheBasics of Grammar — 14

2-1
WHAT IS GRAMMAR?

2-2
THE COMPONENTS OF GRAMMAR

2-3
PRESCRIPTIVE VS. DESCRIPTIVE GRAMMAR

2-4
COMMON GRAMMATICAL TERMINOLOGY

3   Parts ofSpeech — 31

3-1

NOUNS

3-2
PRONOUNS

3-3
VERBS

3-4
ADJECTIVES

3-5
ADVERBS

3-6
PREPOSITIONS

3-7
CONJUNCTIONS

3-8
INTERJECTIONS

   SentenceStructure   65

4-1
SUBJECT AND PREDICATE

4-2
TYPES OF SENTENCES

4-3
SENTENCE FRAGMENTS AND RUN-ON SENTENCES

4-4
SENTENCE CLAUSES

4-5
SENTENCE TYPES IN TESOL

      5   Tenses and Verb Forms   82

5-1

UNDERSTANDING VERB TENSES

5-2
SIMPLE TENSES

5-3
PERFECT TENSES

5-4 Progressive tenses 91

5-5
PERFECT PROGRESSIVE TENSES

5-6
IRREGULAR VERBS

5-7
TEACHING VERB TENSES EFFECTIVELY

6 Articles and Determiners 103

6-1
ARTICLES (A, AN, THE)

6-2
DEMONSTRATIVES

6-3
QUANTIFIERS

6-4
POSSESSIVE DETERMINERS

7 Adjectives and Adverbs 121

7-1
USING ADJECTIVES

7-2
USING ADVERBS

7-3

DEGREES OF COMPARISON

7-4
COMMON ADJECTIVE AND ADVERB ERRORS

8 — Pronouns and Agreement — 139

8-1
PERSONAL PRONOUNS

8-2
DEMONSTRATIVE PRONOUNS

8-3
INDEFINITE PRONOUNS

8-4
REFLEXIVE PRONOUNS

8-5
PRONOUN-ANTECEDENT AGREEMENT

8-6
AVOIDING PRONOUN AMBIGUITY

9 — Prepositions and Phrasal Verbs — 160

9-1
COMMON PREPOSITIONS

9-2
PREPOSITIONAL PHRASES

9-3
PREPOSITIONS OF TIME, PLACE, AND MOVEMENT

9-4
PHRASAL VERBS: UNDERSTANDING AND TEACHING THEM

10 — Conjunctions and Connectors — 178

10-1

COORDINATING CONJUNCTIONS

10-2
SUBORDINATING CONJUNCTIONS

10-3
CORRELATIVE CONJUNCTIONS

10-4
CONNECTORS IN WRITING AND SPEAKING

11 Complex Sentences and Clauses — 198

11-1
DEPENDENT VS. INDEPENDENT CLAUSES

11-2
TYPES OF SUBORDINATE CLAUSES

11-3
COMPLEX SENTENCES IN TESOL

11-4
TEACHING COMPLEX SENTENCES EFFECTIVELY

12 Modal Verbs and Conditional Sentences — 215

12-1
UNDERSTANDING MODAL VERBS

12-2
USING MODAL VERBS IN TESOL

12-3
CONDITIONAL SENTENCES: ZERO, FIRST, SECOND, AND THIRD CONDITIONALS

12-4
TEACHING MODALS AND CONDITIONALS

13 Passive Voice and Reported Speech — 235

13-1

PASSIVE VOICE: FORMATION AND USE

13-2
TEACHING PASSIVE VOICE

13-3
REPORTED SPEECH: DIRECT AND INDIRECT SPEECH

13-4
TEACHING REPORTED SPEECH

14 — Common Grammar Pitfalls — 253

14-1
MOST COMMON ESL GRAMMAR ERRORS

14-2
STRATEGIES FOR ERROR CORRECTION

14-3
PROMPTING SELF-CORRECTION

15 — Teaching Grammar Effectively — 269

15-1
COMMUNICATIVE LANGUAGE TEACHING (CLT)

15-2
INTEGRATING GRAMMAR INTO LESSONS

15-3
USING AUTHENTIC MATERIALS

15-4
INCORPORATING TECHNOLOGY

15-5
ASSESSMENT AND FEEDBACK

16 — Resources and Further Reading — 293

16-1 Recommended Grammar Books — 294

16-2

ONLINE RESOURCES

16-3
PROFESSIONAL ORGANIZATIONS

 Conclusion 304

17-1
THE ONGOING JOURNEY OF GRAMMAR MASTERY IN TESOL

Appendices 309

18-1
GRAMMAR EXERCISES AND ACTIVITIES

18-2
EXERCISE: REPORTED SPEECH PRACTICE

18-3
SAMPLE LESSON PLAN: CONDITIONAL SENTENCE TYPE TWO

18-4
SAMPLE LESSON PLAN: PRESENT PERFECT TENSE

18-5
SAMPLE LESSON PLAN: QUESTION TAGS

18-6
GLOSSARY

Mastering Grammar: A Comprehensive Guide for TESOL Teachers

Mastering Grammar:
A Comprehensive Guide for TESOL Teachers

About the Book

"Mastering Grammar: A Comprehensive Guide for TESOL Teachers" aims to be an indispensable resource for TESOL educators seeking to enhance their understanding of English grammar and effectively transmit this knowledge to their students. By combining a thorough exploration of grammar concepts with practical teaching strategies, this book equips TESOL teachers with the tools they need to help learners achieve proficiency in English grammar.

About the Author

Amir Abbas Ravaei holds a PhD in TESOL and is the founder and CEO of the Vancouver TESOL Training Center in North Vancouver, Canada. He is a Teacher Trainer and Consumer Choice Awards winner for the best language school in Greater Vancouver.

He is also the National Director of the T.I.E.L.C Regional Board of TESOL Authority.

Acknowledgement

I would like to express my deepest gratitude and appreciation to all individuals who have contributed to the successful completion of this book.

Firstly, I would like to thank my family who has been my unwavering support system throughout this journey. Their constant encouragement, love and understanding have been instrumental in making this possible.

I am also grateful to my friends and colleagues who have offered their valuable insights and feedback, helping me to refine my ideas and shape the content of this book.

I would like to extend my heartfelt thanks to my editor, who has provided guidance and expert advice in the writing process. Their knowledge and expertise in the field have been invaluable.

Finally, I would like to thank my publisher, who has believed in this project and provided the necessary resources and support to bring this book to fruition.

Thank you all for your invaluable contributions and unwavering support. This book would not have been possible without your help.

Chapter 1

Introduction

1-1

The Importance of Grammar in TESOL

Grammar plays a crucial role in Teaching English to Speakers of Other Languages (TESOL) for several reasons:

1. **Effective Communication:** Grammar is the backbone of any language, including English. A solid understanding of grammar is essential for learners to communicate effectively, whether they are speaking, listening, reading, or writing. Without proper grammar, learners may struggle to convey their ideas accurately, leading to misunderstandings.

2. **Clarity and Precision:** Proper grammar provides clarity and precision in communication. It helps learners express their thoughts and ideas with accuracy, ensuring that their messages are understood as intended. This is especially important when learners are using English in real-life situations, such as in the workplace or in social interactions.

3. **Confidence Building:** A strong grasp of grammar can boost learners' confidence in using English. When learners are confident in their language skills, they are more likely to participate actively in class and engage in meaningful conversations. This confidence can also extend to other areas of their lives where English is required.

4. **Professional and Academic Success:** In academic and professional settings, grammar errors can have a significant impact on a learner's credibility and success. Academic essays, job applications, and business communication all require proper grammar. Teaching grammar in TESOL equips learners with the language skills they need to excel in these areas.

5. **Cultural Sensitivity:** Learning grammar in TESOL includes understanding cultural nuances and context-appropriate language use. This is particularly important in English, which is spoken and written in various cultural and regional contexts. Teaching grammar within its cultural context helps learners avoid unintended cultural insensitivity.

6. **Language Acquisition:** While some language learning approaches emphasize communication over grammar, a solid understanding of grammar can actually facilitate language acquisition. It provides a framework that helps learners make sense of the language's

structure, making it easier for them to internalize new vocabulary and language patterns.

7. **Standardization:** Teaching grammar helps establish a standard for the English language. While English is a global language with numerous dialects and variations, a standardized form is essential for international communication and for learners to access resources, such as textbooks and educational materials.

8. **Error Correction:** Teaching grammar enables TESOL instructors to effectively correct learners' errors. Constructive feedback on grammar mistakes helps learners identify and rectify their weaknesses, leading to continuous improvement in their language skills.

9. **Building a Foundation:** Grammar is often taught as a foundational skill in language learning. Once learners have a strong grasp of grammar, they can more easily build upon that foundation to develop their vocabulary and language fluency.

In conclusion, grammar is a fundamental component of TESOL. It provides learners with the tools they need to communicate effectively, succeed academically and professionally, and navigate the cultural and social aspects of English-speaking environments. Effective TESOL instruction should strike a balance between teaching grammar and promoting communicative competence to ensure well-rounded language development.

1-2

Understanding the Target Audience

In the context of Teaching English to Speakers of Other Languages (TESOL), studying grammar is an important aspect for several groups of individuals:

1. **TESOL Teachers:** TESOL teachers, whether they are teaching English as a foreign language (EFL) or English as a second language (ESL), should study grammar thoroughly. They need to have a deep understanding of English grammar rules and structures to effectively teach them to their students.

2. **TESOL Teacher Trainees:** Individuals who are undergoing training to become TESOL teachers should study grammar as part of their training program. This is a fundamental component of TESOL certification courses.

3. **Non-Native English Speakers:** Non-native English speakers who aspire to become TESOL teachers or

improve their English language proficiency for other purposes should also study grammar. A strong grasp of grammar helps non-native speakers communicate more effectively and confidently in English.

4. **Language Learners:** While not directly related to TESOL, language learners who are studying English should also study grammar to enhance their language skills. Understanding grammar helps learners communicate accurately and comprehend written and spoken English better.

5. **Curriculum Developers:** Professionals involved in creating TESOL curriculum and materials, such as textbooks, online courses, or lesson plans, should have a sound knowledge of grammar. They need to design materials that align with language learning objectives and grammar standards.

6. **Language Assessment Specialists:** Those involved in developing language proficiency tests and assessments, such as TOEFL or IELTS, should study grammar to ensure that assessments accurately measure a test-taker's grammatical competence.

7. **ESL/EFL Program Administrators:** Administrators of ESL/EFL programs should have an understanding of grammar to make informed decisions about curriculum, teacher training, and program evaluation.

In summary, studying grammar is essential for TESOL teachers, teacher trainees, non-native English speakers, curriculum developers, assessment specialists, and program administrators. It plays a pivotal role in effective language instruction and learning.

Chapter 2

TheBasics of Grammar

2-1

What Is Grammar?

Grammar is the set of rules and principles that govern the structure and composition of a language. It encompasses the way words are organized into sentences, how sentences are structured, and the relationships between different elements in a sentence. Grammar plays a crucial role in communication, as it helps ensure that spoken and written language is clear, coherent, and understandable.

Key aspects of grammar include:

1. **Syntax:** Syntax deals with the arrangement of words to form sentences. It dictates the order of words and phrases to convey meaning. For example, in English, a typical sentence structure is subject-verb-object (SVO), as in "She (subject) reads (verb) a book (object)."

2. **Parts of Speech:** Words are categorized into different parts of speech based on their roles in a sentence. Common parts of speech include nouns (e.g., person, place,

thing), verbs (e.g., action words), adjectives (e.g., describing words), adverbs (e.g., words that modify verbs or adjectives), pronouns (e.g., he, she, it), conjunctions (e.g., and, but), and prepositions (e.g., in, on, under).

3. **Tenses:** Grammar includes rules for expressing the timing of actions or events in a sentence. This is typically done through verb conjugation, such as past tense (e.g., "walked"), present tense (e.g., "walks"), and future tense (e.g., "will walk").

4. **Agreement:** Agreement refers to the need for words in a sentence to match in terms of gender, number, and person. For example, in English, you should say "He is" (third person singular) but "They are" (third person plural).

5. **Punctuation:** Punctuation marks, such as commas, periods, and question marks, are used to indicate pauses, clarify meaning, and structure sentences properly.

6. **Grammar Rules:** These are specific guidelines for using language correctly. Examples include subject-verb agreement, proper use of articles (a, an, the), and avoiding sentence fragments and run-on sentences.

7. **Grammar Variations:** Different languages and dialects have their own unique grammatical rules and variations. Additionally, formal and informal language use may differ in terms of grammar.

8. **Stylistic Elements:** Grammar also includes considerations of style, such as choosing between active and passive voice or varying sentence lengths and structures to create specific effects in writing.

Understanding and following grammar rules is essential for effective communication and writing. It helps convey ideas clearly, prevents misunderstandings, and ensures that language usage is consistent and coherent. While grammar rules can vary from one language to another and may have exceptions, they provide a foundation for language structure and organization.

2-2

The Components of Grammar

Grammar is the set of rules and structures that govern the way we use language to communicate effectively. It consists of several components, each of which plays a crucial role in constructing sentences and conveying meaning. The major components of grammar include:

1. **Syntax:** Syntax refers to the rules governing the structure of sentences in a language. It deals with word order, sentence structure, and how words are combined to form meaningful sentences. Different languages have different syntax rules.

2. **Morphology:** Morphology is the study of the structure of words. It deals with the formation of words, including prefixes, suffixes, and root words, as well as how words change to indicate tense, number, gender, and case. For example, in English, "walk" becomes "walked" in the past tense.

3. **Semantics:** Semantics is the study of meaning in language. It explores how words, phrases, and sentences convey meaning and how different words and structures can have various meanings in different contexts.

4. **Phonology:** Phonology is the study of the sound patterns of a language. It deals with the way sounds function in a particular language, including phonemes (distinctive sound units) and the rules for combining them.

5. **Pragmatics:** Pragmatics focuses on the use of language in context. It involves understanding how people use language to convey meaning beyond the literal interpretation of words. This includes implicature, presupposition, speech acts, and conversational implicature.

6. **Grammar Categories:**

    - **Nouns:** Nouns are words that represent people, places, things, or ideas. They can be singular or plural and often have gender and case forms in some languages.

- **Verbs:** Verbs express actions, states, or events. They conjugate to indicate tense, aspect, mood, and person.

- **Adjectives:** Adjectives describe or modify nouns. They provide additional information about the qualities or characteristics of a noun.

- **Adverbs:** Adverbs modify verbs, adjectives, or other adverbs. They provide information about the manner, time, place, or frequency of an action.

- **Pronouns:** Pronouns replace nouns to avoid repetition. Common pronouns include "he," "she," "it," "they," "you," etc.

- **Conjunctions:** Conjunctions connect words, phrases, or clauses within a sentence. Common conjunctions include "and," "but," "or," "if," "because," etc.

- **Prepositions:** Prepositions show relationships between nouns and other words in a sentence. They indicate location, direction, time, and more. Examples include "in," "on," "under," "with," "to," etc.

- **Articles:** Articles (e.g., "a," "an," "the") are determiners that introduce nouns and help specify whether the noun is definite or indefinite.

These components work together to create meaningful and grammatically correct sentences in a language. Different languages may have variations in their grammar rules and structures, making each language unique in its own way. Understanding and using these components effectively is essential for effective communication in any language.

2-3

Prescriptive vs. Descriptive Grammar

Prescriptive grammar and descriptive grammar are two different approaches to understanding and analyzing language. They serve distinct purposes and have contrasting viewpoints:

1. Prescriptive Grammar:

    - **Purpose**: Prescriptive grammar focuses on providing rules and guidelines for how a language "should" be used. It prescribes norms and standards for language usage.

    - **Authority**: It often reflects the opinions and rules set by language authorities, such as grammar books, language academies, or language teachers.

- **Usage**: Prescriptive grammar is concerned with maintaining and upholding language standards. It aims to establish what is considered correct or proper usage within a language. It often includes rules about grammar, punctuation, syntax, and vocabulary.

- **Example**: Prescriptive grammar might dictate that a sentence should not end with a preposition, even though many native speakers naturally do so.

- **Critique**: Critics argue that prescriptive grammar can be overly rigid and may not account for the evolving nature of language or regional variations. It can also perpetuate linguistic biases and stigmatize certain dialects or ways of speaking.

2. Descriptive Grammar:

- **Purpose**: Descriptive grammar aims to objectively analyze and describe how a language is actually used by its speakers. It seeks to understand and document the natural patterns and structures of a language.

- **Authority**: It relies on linguistic research, observations, and data rather than prescriptive rules. Linguists and language scientists often employ descriptive grammar in their studies.

- **Usage**: Descriptive grammar doesn't make judgments about correct or incorrect language use. Instead, it explores how people communicate, including the variations and nuances found in different dialects, regions, and contexts.

- **Example**: Descriptive grammar would study and describe the grammatical structures and vocabulary used in various English dialects, without labeling any as superior or inferior.

- **Critique**: Critics argue that descriptive grammar can be permissive and may not provide clear guidance for language learners or writers who want to adhere to specific language standards.

In summary, prescriptive grammar provides rules and norms for "correct" language usage, often based on authority and tradition, while descriptive grammar seeks to objectively describe how language is naturally used, without making value judgments. Both approaches have their merits and limitations, and they can be used in different contexts depending on the goals of communication and language study.

2-4

Common Grammatical Terminology

Grammatical terminology refers to the terms and concepts used to describe the structure and rules of a language. Here are some common grammatical terms:

1. **Noun**: A word that represents a person, place, thing, or idea. Examples include "dog," "city," and "love."

2. **Verb**: A word that describes an action, occurrence, or state of being. Examples include "run," "is," and "sing."

3. **Adjective**: A word that modifies a noun, providing more information about it. Examples include "happy," "blue," and "tall."

4. **Adverb**: A word that modifies a verb, adjective, or other adverb, providing information about how, when, where, or to what extent something happens. Examples include "quickly," "very," and "here."

5. **Pronoun**: A word that is used to replace a noun in order to avoid repetition. Examples include "he," "she," "it," and "they."

6. **Preposition**: A word that shows the relationship between a noun (or pronoun) and other words in a sentence. Examples include "in," "on," "under," and "between."

7. **Conjunction**: A word or group of words used to connect words, phrases, or clauses in a sentence. Examples include "and," "but," "or," and "because."

8. **Article**: A type of determiner that comes before a noun and indicates whether the noun is specific or nonspecific. In English, "the" is the definite article, and "a" and "an" are indefinite articles.

9. **Clause**: A group of words that contains a subject and a verb and can stand alone as a sentence (independent clause) or cannot stand alone and depends on an independent clause (dependent clause).

10. **Subject:** The noun, pronoun, or noun phrase that performs the action or is the focus of the sentence.

11. **Predicate:** The part of a sentence that contains the verb and provides information about the subject, often describing what the subject is doing or what is happening to it.

12. **Direct Object:** A noun or pronoun that receives the action of the verb in a sentence.

13. **Indirect Object:** A noun or pronoun that receives the action of the verb indirectly and typically answers the question "to whom" or "for whom" something is done.

14. **Tense:** The grammatical feature that indicates the time of an action or state, such as past, present, or future. English has several tenses, including past, present, and future.

15. **Voice:** The form of a verb that shows whether the subject performs the action (active voice) or receives the action (passive voice).

16. **Mood:** The grammatical feature that indicates the speaker's attitude or the likelihood of an action. Common moods include indicative (states facts), imperative

(gives commands), and subjunctive (expresses hypothetical situations).

17. **Conjugation:** The process of changing the form of a verb to indicate tense, mood, voice, number, and person.

18. **Syntax:** The arrangement of words and phrases to create well-formed sentences in a language.

19. **Phrase:** A group of related words that functions as a single unit within a sentence.

20. **Sentence:** A group of words that expresses a complete thought and typically includes a subject and a predicate.

These are just some of the fundamental grammatical terms used to analyze and describe the structure of language. Understanding these terms can be helpful in studying and discussing the rules of grammar and syntax in a language.

Chapter 3

Parts ofSpeech

3-1

Nouns

Nouns are words that represent people, places, things, or ideas. They are one of the fundamental parts of speech in English and serve as the building blocks of sentences. Nouns can be classified into several categories, including:

1. **Common nouns:** These refer to general, non-specific people, places, things, or ideas. For example, "dog," "city," "book," and "happiness" are common nouns.

2. **Proper nouns:** These are used to refer to specific, individual people, places, or things and are typically capitalized. For instance, "John" (a person), "Paris" (a city), and "The Great Gatsby" (a book) are proper nouns.

3. **Concrete nouns:** These represent physical objects that can be perceived through the senses, such as "tree," "car," and "apple."

4. **Abstract nouns:** These refer to concepts, emotions, qualities, or ideas that are not tangible, like "love," "freedom," "honesty," and "beauty."

5. **Collective nouns:** These denote groups or collections of things, animals, or people, such as "team," "flock," and "family."

6. **Countable nouns:** These are nouns that can be counted and have both singular and plural forms. For example, "dog" (singular) and "dogs" (plural).

7. **Uncountable nouns:** These are nouns that cannot be counted individually and do not have a plural form. They represent substances, concepts, or mass nouns, like "water," "information," and "happiness."

8. **Compound nouns:** These are formed by combining two or more words to create a single noun, like "toothbrush," "breakfast," and "schoolteacher."

9. **Possessive nouns:** These indicate ownership or possession and are formed by adding an apostrophe and an "s" ('s) to the end of a noun, as in "Sarah's car" or "the company's profits."

Nouns play a crucial role in sentence structure, serving as subjects, objects, and complements. They can also be modified by adjectives and determiners to provide more context and detail within a sentence.

3-2

Pronouns

Pronouns are words used in language to replace nouns and noun phrases, making sentences less repetitive and more concise. Pronouns are an essential part of communication and help to clarify who or what is being referred to in a sentence. Here are some common types of pronouns:

1. **Personal Pronouns:** Personal pronouns are used to refer to specific people or things. They can change depending on the person (first, second, or third), number (singular or plural), and gender (masculine, feminine, or neuter). Examples include:
   - First person singular: I, me, my, mine
   - Second person singular: you, your, yours
   - Third person singular: he, him, his (masculine), she, her, hers (feminine), it, its (neuter)

2. **Possessive Pronouns:** Possessive pronouns indicate ownership or possession. They include:
   - First person singular: mine

- Second person singular: yours
- Third person singular: his (masculine), hers (feminine), its (neuter)
- First person plural: ours
- Second person plural: yours
- Third person plural: theirs

3. **Reflexive Pronouns:** Reflexive pronouns are used when the subject and object of a sentence are the same person or thing. They end in "-self" (singular) or "-selves" (plural). Examples include:
    - Singular: myself, yourself, himself, herself, itself
    - Plural: ourselves, yourselves, themselves

4. **Relative Pronouns:** Relative pronouns introduce relative clauses (clauses that provide more information about a noun). Common relative pronouns include:
    - who (referring to people)
    - which (referring to things or animals)
    - that (referring to both people and things)

5. **Interrogative Pronouns:** Interrogative pronouns are used to ask questions. Common interrogative pronouns include:
    - who (asking about people)
    - whom (asking about the object of an action)
    - what (asking about things)

6. **Demonstrative Pronouns:** Demonstrative pronouns are used to point to specific things or people. They include:
    - this (singular, close proximity)
    - these (plural, close proximity)
    - that (singular, farther proximity)
    - those (plural, farther proximity)

7. **Indefinite Pronouns:** Indefinite pronouns refer to non-specific or unidentified people or things. Examples include:
    - all, another, any, anybody, anyone, both, each, either, everybody, everyone, everything, few, many, neither, nobody, no one, none, nothing, several, some, somebody, someone, something

8. **Reciprocal Pronouns:** Reciprocal pronouns indicate an action that is reciprocated or shared between two or more people or things. Examples include:
    - each other
    - one another

Pronouns play a crucial role in language and are used to avoid repetition, maintain clarity, and create more efficient communication.

3-3

Verbs

Verbs are one of the fundamental parts of speech in English and many other languages. They are words that describe actions, occurrences, or states of being. Verbs are essential for constructing sentences and conveying meaning. Here are some key points about verbs:

1. **Action Verbs**: These verbs describe physical or mental actions. For example: "run," "think," "jump."

2. **State of Being Verbs (Linking Verbs)**: These verbs connect the subject of a sentence to a subject complement or adjective that describes or renames the subject. The most common linking verb is "to be" in its various forms (am, is, are, was, were, etc.). For example: "She is happy."

3. **Transitive Verbs**: These verbs require a direct object to complete their meaning. For example: "She ate the cake." In this sentence, "ate" is the transitive verb, and "cake" is the direct object.

4. **Intransitive Verbs**: These verbs do not require a direct object to complete their meaning. For example: "He sleeps." In this sentence, "sleeps" is an intransitive verb.

5. **Auxiliary Verbs (Modal Verbs)**: These verbs, such as "can," "will," "should," "must," are used in combination with main verbs to express various shades of meaning like possibility, necessity, or permission. For example: "She can sing."

6. **Regular Verbs**: These verbs form their past tense and past participle by adding "-ed" to the base form. For example: "walk" (base form), "walked" (past tense), "walked" (past participle).

7. **Irregular Verbs**: These verbs do not follow the regular pattern of adding "-ed" to form their past tense and past participle. They have unique forms. For example: "go" (base form), "went" (past tense), "gone" (past participle).

8. **Tense**: Verbs can be used in different tenses to indicate when an action or state of being occurred. The common tenses include present, past, and future tenses, as well as various perfect and progressive forms.

9. **Voice**: Verbs can be in either active or passive voice. In active voice, the subject performs the action. In passive voice, the subject receives the action.

10. **Mood**: Verbs can express different moods, such as indicative (stating a fact), imperative (giving a command), subjunctive (expressing a hypothetical or unreal condition), and conditional (expressing something contingent on another event).

11. **Infinitive**: The base form of a verb is called the infinitive. In English, infinitives are often preceded by "to," as in "to eat," "to swim."

12. **Gerunds**: These are verbs that function as nouns and end in "-ing." For example, in "Swimming is my favorite hobby," "swimming" is a gerund.

13. **Participles**: These are verb forms that can function as adjectives. There are present participles (ending in "-ing") and past participles (often ending in "-ed" or irregular forms). For example, in "The broken window," "broken" is a past participle used as an adjective.

14. **Infinitive Phrases**: These are phrases that consist of an infinitive verb and any accompanying words

or phrases. For example, "to study for the exam" is an infinitive phrase.

15. **Phrasal Verbs**: These are verbs formed by combining a main verb with one or more particles (usually prepositions or adverbs), resulting in a different meaning. For example, "give up" or "look after."

Verbs play a crucial role in sentence construction and convey the action or state of being in a sentence. They are an essential element of effective communication in both spoken and written language.

3-4

Adjectives

Adjectives are a category of words used to describe or modify nouns (people, places, things, or ideas) in a sentence. They provide more information about the noun, helping to make the text more descriptive and expressive. Adjectives can describe various qualities or characteristics of the noun they modify. Here are some examples of adjectives:

1. **Descriptive Adjectives:** These adjectives provide details about the noun's physical or qualitative attributes.
    - **Beautiful** flowers
    - **Blue** sky
    - **Tall** building
    - **Delicious** pizza

2. **Quantitative Adjectives:** These adjectives indicate the quantity or how much of the noun is being referred to.
    - **Many** books
    - **Few** people
    - **Several** opportunities

- One apple

3. **Demonstrative Adjectives:** These adjectives point to a specific noun and include words like "this," "that," "these," and "those."
   - I like **this** shirt.
   - Are you interested in **those** cars?

4. **Possessive Adjectives:** These adjectives show ownership or possession and include words like "my," "your," "his," "her," "its," "our," and "their."
   - **My** house is big.
   - **Their** dog is friendly.

5. **Interrogative Adjectives:** These adjectives are used to ask questions and include words like "which," "what," and "whose."
   - **What** book are you reading?
   - **Whose** bag is this?

6. **Numeral Adjectives:** These adjectives indicate the number or order of the noun, including words like "first," "second," "three," "fourth," etc.
   - She is the **third** person in line.
   - The **four** seasons are beautiful.

7. **Exclamatory Adjectives:** These adjectives express strong emotion and are often followed by an exclamation mark.

- **Amazing** sunset!
- **Incredible** performance!

8. **Comparative and Superlative Adjectives:** These adjectives are used to compare two or more things. They include words like "better," "best," "worse," "worst," "bigger," "biggest," etc.
    - This is the **best** movie I've seen.
    - She is **smarter** than her brother.

9. **Adjectives of Color:** These adjectives describe the color of the noun.
    - The walls are **red**.
    - He wore a **green** shirt.

10. **Adjectives of Size:** These adjectives indicate the size of the noun.
    - The cat is **small**.
    - It's a **huge** mountain.

Adjectives play a crucial role in providing vivid descriptions and adding depth to sentences. They help convey sensory information and enable writers to paint a more detailed picture for readers or listeners.

In English, adjectives are used to describe or modify nouns. When multiple adjectives are used to describe the same noun, they generally follow a specific order or sequence. This order is not strict, but it is commonly observed to make the sentence sound more natural and understandable. The general order of adjectives in English is as follows:

1. **Opinion:** Adjectives that express the speaker's opinion or evaluation of the noun.
     - Examples: beautiful, ugly, nice, delicious, wonderful

2. **Size:** Adjectives that indicate the size of the noun.
     - Examples: small, large, tiny, enormous, huge

3. **Age:** Adjectives that describe the age of the noun.
     - Examples: old, young, new, ancient

4. **Shape:** Adjectives that specify the shape of the noun.
     - Examples: round, square, triangular, oval

5. **Color:** Adjectives that indicate the color of the noun.
     - Examples: red, blue, green, yellow, black

6. **Origin:** Adjectives that denote the origin or source of the noun.
     - Examples: American, French, Chinese, wooden (referring to material)

7. **Material:** Adjectives that describe the material composition of the noun.
     - Examples: wooden, metal, plastic, silk

8. **Purpose or Qualifier:** Adjectives that clarify the purpose or use of the noun.

- Examples: cooking (as in "cooking pot"), wedding (as in "wedding dress"), swimming (as in "swimming pool")

9. **Noun:** The noun that the adjectives are modifying.

Here are some examples of how these adjectives might be used in a sentence:

- She has a **beautiful** (opinion) **old** (age) **round** (shape) **wooden** (material) **table**.
- He bought a **large** (size) **red** (color) **Italian** (origin) **sports** (purpose) **car**.

It's important to note that not all adjectives will fit neatly into this order, and in some cases, you might use multiple adjectives from the same category to provide more detailed descriptions.

Additionally, native speakers might not always follow this order rigidly, especially in casual conversation. However, adhering to this order generally helps in making your sentences more coherent and natural-sounding.

3-5

Adverbs

Adverbs are a type of word that modify or describe verbs, adjectives, other adverbs, or even entire sentences. They provide additional information about how, when, where, why, or to what degree an action is performed. Adverbs can add depth and clarity to a sentence, helping readers or listeners understand the details of an action or event.

Here are some common types of adverbs:

1. **Adverbs of Manner:** These adverbs describe how an action is performed. They often end in "-ly." For example, "She sang beautifully."

2. **Adverbs of Time:** These adverbs indicate when an action takes place or the frequency of an action. Examples include "now," "soon," "daily," and "often."

3. **Adverbs of Place:** These adverbs describe the location or direction of an action. Examples include "here," "there," "everywhere," and "above."

4. **Adverbs of Frequency:** These adverbs specify how often an action occurs. Examples include "always," "sometimes," "rarely," and "never."

5. **Adverbs of Degree:** These adverbs modify adjectives or other adverbs to indicate the extent or degree of an action. Examples include "very," "too," "almost," and "quite."

6. **Adverbs of Certainty:** These adverbs express the speaker's level of confidence or certainty about a statement. Examples include "definitely," "probably," and "certainly."

7. **Adverbs of Purpose:** These adverbs explain why an action is performed. Examples include "to," "in order to," and "so as to."

8. **Interrogative Adverbs:** These adverbs are used to ask questions about various aspects of an action, such as "when," "where," "why," and "how."

Here are some example sentences using adverbs:

- She danced gracefully (adverb of manner).
- They arrived late (adverb of time).

- He looked everywhere for his keys (adverb of place).
- She often goes jogging in the morning (adverb of frequency).
- The food was too spicy for my taste (adverb of degree).
- I am definitely going to the party (adverb of certainty).
- He studied hard to pass the exam (adverb of purpose).
- When did you arrive? (interrogative adverb)

Using adverbs effectively in your writing or speech can make your communication more precise and engaging by providing additional context and nuance. However, it's important not to overuse adverbs, as excessive adverbial modifiers can make your writing verbose and less impactful.

3-6

Prepositions

Prepositions are words that typically show the relationship between two words or phrases in a sentence. They often indicate location, direction, time, or relationships between objects or ideas. Prepositions are important for clarifying the spatial and temporal aspects of a sentence. Here are some common prepositions in English:

1. **In:** Used to indicate location within an enclosed space or a time frame.
     - She is in the house.
     - The meeting is in an hour.

2. **On:** Used to indicate location on a surface or a specific day/date.
     - The book is on the table.
     - We will meet on Monday.

3. **At:** Used to indicate a specific point in time or a specific location.
     - He arrived at 3 o'clock.

- They are waiting at the bus stop.

4. **Under:** Indicates location below or beneath something.
   - The cat is under the table.
   - The treasure is buried under the ground.

5. **Over:** Indicates movement from one side to another, or a position higher than something.
   - The plane flew over the mountains.
   - Hang the picture over the fireplace.

6. **Between:** Used to indicate a relationship or position in the middle of two things.
   - She is sitting between Tom and Jerry.
   - The park is located between two tall buildings.

7. **Among:** Similar to "between" but used when there are more than two things.
   - Among the flowers in the garden, a single rose stood out.

8. **Through:** Indicates movement from one side to the other or passing from one point to another.
   - The car drove through the tunnel.
   - She read through the entire book.

9. **With:** Indicates association, accompaniment, or the instrument used.

- I went to the store with my friend.
- Cut the bread with a knife.

10. **For:** Used to indicate purpose, duration, or recipient.
    - She bought a gift for her sister.
    - They talked for hours.
11. **By:** Indicates means, method, or agent of an action.
    - The letter was delivered by mail.
    - He fixed the problem by using a wrench.

12. **To:** Indicates movement or direction toward a place or person.
    - They went to the park.
    - Give this gift to your mother.
13. **Of:** Often indicates possession, composition, or origin.
    - The book of Mark.
    - The dress is made of silk.

14. **For:** Used to indicate purpose, duration, or recipient.
    - She bought a gift for her sister.
    - They talked for hours.

These are just a few examples of common prepositions in English. There are many more prepositions, and their usage can vary depending on the context and the specific meaning they convey in a sentence. Understanding prepositions is essential for constructing clear and grammatically correct sentences in English.

3-7

Conjunctions

Conjunctions are words or groups of words that connect phrases, clauses, or sentences in a sentence. They serve to show the relationship between the connected parts of a sentence. Conjunctions can be categorized into several types:

1. **Coordinating Conjunctions:** These connect words, phrases, or clauses of equal importance. The most common coordinating conjunctions are often remembered using the acronym FANBOYS:
    - For (used to explain reasons)
    - And (used to connect similar ideas)
    - Nor (used to indicate a negative alternative)
    - But (used to introduce a contrast or exception)
    - Or (used to indicate alternatives)
    - Yet (used to introduce a contrasting idea)
    - So (used to show result or consequence) Example: I wanted pizza, but she preferred

2. **Subordinating Conjunctions:** These connect a dependent (subordinate) clause to an independent clause,

creating complex sentences. Subordinating conjunctions indicate the relationship between the two clauses, such as cause and effect, time, condition, or contrast.

Example: Because it was raining, we stayed indoors.

1. **Correlative Conjunctions:** These are pairs of conjunctions that work together to connect elements in a sentence. Common examples include "either...or," "neither...nor," "both...and," and "not only...but "

Example: She can either go to the party or stay home.

1. **Conjunctive Adverbs:** These are adverbs that also function as conjunctions. They are used to connect independent clauses and typically show relationships such as contrast, cause and effect, or sequence. Some common conjunctive adverbs include "however," "therefore," "meanwhile," and "consequently."

Example: He studied hard; consequently, he aced the exam.

1. **Relative Pronouns:** While not always considered traditional conjunctions, relative pronouns like "who," "which," and "that" can be used to connect relative clauses to the main clause. They introduce additional information about a noun in the main

Example: The book that I'm reading is very interesting.

1. Coordinating and Subordinating Conjunctions in Lists: Conjunctions like "and" and "or" are often used in lists to connect three or more

Example: I need to buy apples, bananas, and oranges.

Remember that the choice of conjunction can significantly impact the meaning and flow of a sentence, so it's essential to use them correctly and consider the relationships between the elements they connect.

3-8

Interjections

Interjections are words or phrases that express strong emotions, reactions, or exclamations in a sentence. They are typically used to convey feelings such as surprise, excitement, anger, joy, or frustration. Interjections are often standalone words or short phrases and are not grammatically connected to the rest of the sentence. They are used to add emphasis or convey the speaker's emotional state. Here are some common examples of interjections:

1. **Wow!** - Expressing amazement or astonishment.
2. **Oh no!** - Conveying disappointment or concern.
3. **Yay!** - Expressing joy or excitement.
4. **Ouch!** - Indicating pain or discomfort.
5. **Oops!** - Acknowledging a mistake or accident.
6. **Ah!** - Signifying realization or understanding.
7. **Phew!** - Expressing relief.
8. **Ugh!** - Conveying frustration or disgust.
9. **Hurray!** - Showing enthusiasm or celebration.
10. **Shh!** - Requesting silence or quiet.

Interjections are often used in informal spoken language and in writing to add emotional nuance to a sentence. They can also be used to engage the listener or reader more effectively by conveying the speaker's feelings or reactions. The choice of interjection can greatly influence the tone and mood of a conversation or text.

Chapter 4

SentenceStructure

4-1

Subject and Predicate

In English grammar, a sentence is typically composed of two main parts: the subject and the predicate. These parts work together to convey meaning in a sentence.

1. Subject:
    - The subject is the main noun or pronoun in the sentence that performs the action or is the focus of the sentence.
    - It answers the question "Who?" or "What?" the sentence is about.
    - The subject can be a single word or a group of words acting as a single unit.
    - Examples of subjects:
        - Mary (a single noun)
        - The cat and the dog (a group of words acting as a single unit)
        - She (a pronoun representing a person)

2. Predicate:

- The predicate is the part of the sentence that contains the verb and provides information about the action or state of the subject.
- It answers the question "What does the subject do?" or "What is happening to the subject?"
- The predicate can also include other elements like objects, adverbs, and prepositional phrases that provide additional information about the action or state.
- Examples of predicates:
    - ate lunch (a simple verb phrase)
    - is sleeping (a verb phrase with an auxiliary verb)
    - quickly and with enthusiasm (adverbs modifying the verb)

Here are some examples of complete sentences with both subject and predicate:

1. Mary (subject) laughed (predicate).
2. The cat and the dog (subject) chased (predicate) the squirrel (object).
3. They (subject) have been working (predicate) diligently (adverb) all day.

Understanding the subject and predicate in a sentence is essential for constructing clear and grammatically correct sentences in English.

4-2

Types of Sentences

In English grammar, there are four main types of sentences: declarative, interrogative, imperative, and exclamatory. Each type serves a different purpose and conveys information in a specific way:

1. Declarative Sentences:
    - Purpose: Declarative sentences are used to make statements or convey information. They provide facts, opinions, or descriptions.
    - Example: She loves to read books.

2. Interrogative Sentences:
    - Purpose: Interrogative sentences are used to ask questions and seek information. They typically begin with question words (who, what, when, where, why, how) or with a helping verb (is, are, do, have, can, etc.).
    - Example: Where is the nearest bookstore?

3. Imperative Sentences:
    - Purpose: Imperative sentences are used to give commands, make requests, or offer invitations. They often begin with a verb, and the subject (usually "you") is implied.
    - Example: Please pass me the salt.

4. Exclamatory Sentences:
    - Purpose: Exclamatory sentences are used to express strong emotions, surprise, excitement, or other intense feelings. They typically end with an exclamation mark.
    - Example: What a beautiful sunset!

Additionally, sentences can be classified based on their structure into simple, compound, complex, or compound-complex sentences:

1. Simple Sentences:
    - A simple sentence consists of one independent clause, which contains a subject and a predicate.
    - Example: He walked to the store.

2. Compound Sentences:
    - A compound sentence consists of two or more independent clauses joined together by coordinating conjunctions (e.g., and, but, or) or semicolons.

- Example: She wanted to go to the movies, but I preferred to stay home.

3. Complex Sentences:
    - A complex sentence contains one independent clause and at least one dependent (subordinate) clause. Dependent clauses cannot stand alone as sentences.
    - Example: After I finish my homework, I will watch TV.

4. Compound-Complex Sentences:
    - A compound-complex sentence combines elements of both compound and complex sentences. It has two or more independent clauses and at least one dependent clause.
    - Example: I went to the store, but I forgot to buy milk because I was in a hurry.

Understanding the different types and structures of sentences is essential for effective communication in English. Each type serves a unique purpose and helps convey information in a clear and organized manner.

4-3

Sentence Fragments and Run-On Sentences

Sentence fragments and run-on sentences are two common errors in English grammar. They both involve issues with sentence structure, but they are distinct in their nature.

1. **Sentence Fragments:**
     - A sentence fragment is an incomplete sentence that cannot stand on its own as a complete thought. It's usually missing a subject, a verb, or both.
     - Fragments often occur when a writer mistakenly separates a dependent clause or phrase from the main clause.
     - Example fragments:
         - "Although I tried."
         - "Because he was late for the bus."
           To correct sentence fragments, you need to either add the missing components to make them complete sentences or

incorporate them into a nearby complete sentence.
- Corrected fragments:
    - "Although I tried, I couldn't open the jar."
    - "Because he was late for the bus, he missed his morning meeting."

2. **Run-On Sentences:**
    - A run-on sentence occurs when two or more independent clauses (complete thoughts) are joined together without the appropriate punctuation or conjunctions to separate them.
    - Run-on sentences can be excessively long and confusing, making it hard for readers to follow the writer's intended meaning.
    - Example run-on sentences:
        - "I wanted to go to the movies I didn't have enough money."
        - "She studied all night she still didn't feel prepared for the test." To correct run-on sentences, you have a few options:
    - Use a semicolon to separate the independent clauses: "I wanted to go to the movies; I didn't have enough money."
    - Use a comma and a coordinating conjunction (and, but, or, nor, for, so, yet) to join the clauses: "I wanted to go to the movies, but I didn't have enough money."
    - Create two separate sentences: "I wanted to go to the movies. I didn't have enough money."

Remember that clear and well-structured sentences are essential for effective communication in writing. Careful proofreading and editing can help you avoid both sentence fragments and run-on sentences in your writing.

4-4

Sentence Clauses

A sentence clause, also known as a clause, is a group of words that contains a subject and a predicate and can express a complete thought. Clauses are the building blocks of sentences, and they can be categorized into two main types: independent clauses and dependent clauses.

1. Independent Clause: An independent clause is a group of words that can stand alone as a complete sentence because it expresses a complete thought. It has a subject and a predicate. For example:
    - "She is reading a book."

2. Dependent Clause: A dependent clause, also called a subordinate clause, is a group of words that contains a subject and a predicate but cannot stand alone as a complete sentence because it does not express a complete thought. It relies on an independent clause to form a complete sentence. For example:
    - "Because she is interested in history,"

When you combine an independent clause with one or more dependent clauses, you create complex sentences. Here's an example of a complex sentence:

- "Because she is interested in history, she is reading a book."

  In this complex sentence, "Because she is interested in history" is the dependent clause, and "she is reading a book" is the independent clause.

  Additionally, you can further classify clauses based on their functions within a sentence:

- Main Clause: An independent clause that can stand alone as a sentence.
- Subordinate Clause: A dependent clause that cannot stand alone and depends on a main clause.
- Adjective Clause: A subordinate clause that functions as an adjective to modify a noun.
- Adverbial Clause: A subordinate clause that functions as an adverb to modify a verb, adjective, or adverb.
- Noun Clause: A subordinate clause that functions as a noun within a sentence.

Understanding and using different types of clauses allows you to construct more varied and complex sentences in your writing and communication.

4-5

Sentence Types in TESOL

In Teaching English to Speakers of Other Languages (TESOL), instructors often focus on teaching various sentence types to help students develop their language skills and communication abilities. There are several fundamental sentence types in English, and teaching them effectively is essential for language learners. Here are some common sentence types in TESOL:

1. Declarative Sentences:
    - These sentences make statements or declarations.
    - Example: "She is a teacher."

2. Interrogative Sentences:
    - These sentences ask questions.
    - Example: "Are you coming to the party?"

3. Imperative Sentences:
    - These sentences give commands or instructions.

- Example: "Please close the door."

4. **Exclamatory Sentences:**
    - These sentences express strong emotions or exclamations.
    - Example: "What a beautiful sunset!"

5. **Conditional Sentences:**
    - These sentences express a condition and its potential result.
    - Example: "If it rains, we will stay indoors."

6. **Complex Sentences:**
    - These sentences contain a main clause and one or more subordinate (dependent) clauses.
    - Example: "Although it was raining, they went for a walk."

7. **Compound Sentences:**
    - These sentences consist of two or more independent clauses joined by coordinating conjunctions.
    - Example: "I wanted to go to the movies, but I didn't have enough money."

8. **Passive Sentences:**
    - These sentences focus on the action's receiver rather than the doer.
    - Example: "The book was read by him."

9. Reported (Indirect) Speech:
    - These sentences report what someone else has said.
    - Example: "She said that she was going to the store."

10. Wh-Questions:
    - These questions typically start with who, what, when, where, why, or how.
    - Example: "What time is the meeting?"

11. Tag Questions:
    - These are short questions added to the end of a statement to seek confirmation.
    - Example: "You're coming to the party, aren't you?"

12. Relative Clauses:
    - These clauses provide additional information about a noun.
    - Example: "The person who called is my cousin."

Teaching these sentence types in TESOL involves explaining their structure, usage, and providing opportunities for practice through exercises and real-life communication. Different sentence types serve various communicative functions, and helping students understand and use them effectively is crucial for their language proficiency development.

Chapter 5

Tenses and Verb Forms

5-1

Understanding Verb Tenses

Understanding verb tenses is essential for effective communication in English, as they indicate when an action took place or its relationship to the present and future. English has several verb tenses, including simple, continuous (progressive), perfect, and perfect continuous tenses. Here's an overview of the main verb tenses:

1. Simple Present Tense:
    - Used for actions that are habitual, general facts, or truths.
    - Formed using the base form of the verb.
    - Example: She reads books regularly.

2. Simple Past Tense:
    - Used for actions that happened and were completed in the past.
    - Typically formed by adding "-ed" to regular verbs.
    - Example: They visited Paris last summer.

3. Simple Future Tense:
    - Used to describe actions that will happen in the future.
    - Typically formed using "will" or "shall" with the base form of the verb.
    - Example: He will arrive tomorrow.

4. Present Continuous (Progressive) Tense:
    - Used for actions happening at the present moment or around now.
    - Formed using a form of "to be" (am, is, are) and the base form of the verb with "- ing" added.
    - Example: They are playing soccer right now.

5. Past Continuous (Progressive) Tense:
    - Used for actions that were ongoing in the past.
    - Formed using a past form of "to be" (was, were) and the base form of the verb with "-ing" added.
    - Example: She was studying when the phone rang.

6. Future Continuous (Progressive) Tense:
    - Used for actions that will be ongoing in the future.
    - Formed using "will be" or "shall be" and the base form of the verb with "-ing" added.
    - Example: At 8 PM tonight, I will be watching a movie.

7. Present Perfect Tense:
    - Used to describe actions that happened at an unspecified time before now.
    - Formed using "have" or "has" with the past participle of the verb.
    - Example: I have visited that museum before.

8. Past Perfect Tense:
    - Used to describe an action that occurred before another past action.
    - Formed using "had" with the past participle of the verb.
    - Example: She had finished her homework when her friend called.

9. Future Perfect Tense:
    - Used to describe an action that will be completed before a specified future time.
    - Formed using "will have" or "shall have" with the past participle of the verb.
    - Example: By next year, they will have graduated.

10. Present Perfect Continuous (Progressive) Tense:
    - Used to describe actions that started in the past and continue into the present.
    - Formed using "have been" or "has been" and the base form of the verb with "-ing" added.
    - Example: I have been working here for five years.

11. Past Perfect Continuous (Progressive) Tense:

- Used to describe actions that were ongoing in the past and continued up to a certain point in the past.
- Formed using "had been" and the base form of the verb with "-ing" added.
- Example: He had been studying for hours before he took a break.

12. Future Perfect Continuous (Progressive) Tense:
    - Used to describe actions that will be ongoing and will be completed before a specified future time.
    - Formed using "will have been" and the base form of the verb with "-ing" added.
    - Example: By 5 PM, they will have been working for eight hours.

Understanding when and how to use these verb tenses is crucial for clear and accurate communication in English. It helps convey the timing and duration of actions in both spoken and written language.

5-2

Simple Tenses

Simple tenses are a set of verb tenses in English that are used to describe actions or states of being in a straightforward and uncomplicated manner. There are three main simple tenses in English: the simple present, the simple past, and the simple future. Here's an overview of each:

1. Simple Present Tense:
    - Usage: The simple present tense is used to describe actions or situations that are habitual, regular, or generally true.
    - Form: For most verbs, it is formed by using the base form of the verb (e.g., "I eat," "She reads").
    - Examples:
        - He plays soccer every Saturday.
        - She lives in New York.
        - Water boils at 100 degrees Celsius.

2. Simple Past Tense:
    - Usage: The simple past tense is used to describe completed actions or events that occurred in the past.

- Form: Regular verbs form the simple past by adding '-ed' to the base form (e.g., "I walked," "She talked"). Irregular verbs have unique past tense forms (e.g., "I went," "She ate").
- Examples:
    - I visited Paris last summer.
    - They watched a movie yesterday.
    - She sang beautifully at the concert.

3. **Simple Future Tense:**
    - Usage: The simple future tense is used to describe actions or events that will happen in the future.
    - Form: It is often formed using the auxiliary verb "will" followed by the base form of the verb (e.g., "I will go," "She will study").
    - Examples:
        - I will call you tomorrow.
        - They will visit their grandparents next weekend.
        - She will start her new job in January.

Simple tenses are the most basic forms of expressing time in English, and they serve as the foundation for more complex tenses like the present continuous, past perfect, and future perfect, which provide additional details and nuances about the timing and duration of actions.

5-3

Perfect tenses

Perfect tenses are verb forms in English that indicate an action or state of being that is completed relative to a certain point in time. There are three main perfect tenses in English: the present perfect, the past perfect (also known as the pluperfect), and the future perfect. Each of these tenses has a specific structure and usage:

1. Present Perfect:
    - Structure: [have/has + past participle]
    - Example: I have visited London.
    - Usage: The present perfect tense is used to describe actions or situations that began in the past and have a connection to the present. It emphasizes the result or completion of the action rather than when it occurred.

2. Past Perfect (Pluperfect):
    - Structure: [had + past participle]
    - Example: She had already eaten when I arrived.
    - Usage: The past perfect tense is used to indicate that an action or event was completed

before another past action or point in time. It helps establish a clear sequence of events in the past.

3. **Future Perfect:**
    - Structure: [will have + past participle]
    - Example: By next year, they will have graduated from college.
    - Usage: The future perfect tense is used to express the completion of an action or event at a specified point in the future. It shows that the action will be finished before that future time.

In each of these tenses, the past participle of the verb is used to form the perfect aspect of the verb. Regular verbs typically form the past participle by adding "-ed" to the base form (e.g., "talk" becomes "talked"), while irregular verbs have unique past participle forms (e.g., "go" becomes "gone").

It's important to note that perfect tenses are used to emphasize the completion of an action or event in relation to a specific point in time. They are particularly useful for indicating the order of events in narratives and for discussing actions with relevance to the present or future.

Chapter 5-4

Progressive tenses

Progressive tenses, also known as continuous tenses, are verb tenses used to describe ongoing actions or events that are in progress at a specific point in time. There are three progressive tenses in English: the present progressive, the past progressive, and the future progressive.

1. **Present Progressive:** This tense is used to describe actions or events that are happening right now or around the current time. It is formed by using the present tense of the verb "to be" (am, is, are) and adding the base form of the main verb with the "-ing" suffix.
    - Examples:
        - She **is reading** a book.
        - They **are playing** soccer.

2. **Past Progressive:** This tense is used to describe actions or events that were ongoing in the past at a specific moment or during a specific period. It is formed by using the past tense of the verb "to be" (was, were)

and adding the base form of the main verb with the "-ing" suffix.
- Examples:
    - He **was studying** when the phone rang.
    - We **were watching** a movie last night.

3. **Future Progressive:** This tense is used to describe actions or events that will be in progress at a specific time in the future. It is formed by using the future tense of the verb "to be" (will be) and adding the base form of the main verb with the "-ing" suffix.
    - Examples:
        - Tomorrow, she **will be traveling** to Paris.
        - At this time next year, they **will be living** in a new house.

Progressive tenses are versatile and can be used to provide more context and detail to your sentences, especially when you want to emphasize the ongoing nature of an action or event. They are commonly used in both spoken and written English to convey a sense of time and continuity.

5-5

Perfect Progressive Tenses

The perfect progressive tenses are a group of verb tenses in English that express actions or states that are ongoing, continuous, or repetitive in the past, present, or future, while also emphasizing their duration or the fact that they are completed up to a certain point in time. There are three perfect progressive tenses in English: the present perfect progressive, the past perfect progressive, and the future perfect progressive.

1. **Present Perfect Progressive:**
    - Form: Subject + have/has + been + present participle (-ing form of the verb)
    - Use: This tense is used to describe actions or events that began in the past, are still ongoing in the present, and may continue into the future.
    - Example: She has been studying English for three years.

2. **Past Perfect Progressive:**

- Form: Subject + had + been + past participle (-ing form of the verb)
- Use: This tense is used to describe actions or events that were ongoing in the past and were completed up to a certain point in the past.
- Example: By the time I arrived, they had been waiting for an hour.

3. Future Perfect Progressive:
    - Form: Subject + will have + been + present participle (-ing form of the verb)
    - Use: This tense is used to describe actions or events that will be ongoing in the future and will have been continuing up to a certain point in the future.
    - Example: By next year, she will have been working here for a decade.

In each of these tenses, you use the auxiliary verbs "have," "has," or "had" to form the perfect aspect, "been" to form the progressive aspect, and the present participle or past participle form of the main verb to show ongoing or continuous action. The choice of "have" or "had" depends on whether you're referring to the present, past, or future.

These tenses are useful for providing additional context and nuance to actions or events, especially when you want to emphasize their duration or when they started or ended.

5-6

Irregular verbs

Irregular verbs are verbs in English that do not follow the regular pattern when conjugated in different tenses. While regular verbs typically add "-ed" to the base form to create past tense and past participle forms, irregular verbs have unique forms for these tenses. Here are some common irregular verbs with their base form, past tense, and past participle forms:

1. Go

- Base form: Go
- Past tense: Went
- Past participle: Gone

2. Be

- Base form: Be
- Past tense: Was/Were
- Past participle: Been

3. Have

- Base form: Have
- Past tense: Had
- Past participle: Had

4. Do

- Base form: Do
- Past tense: Did
- Past participle: Done

5. Eat

- Base form: Eat
- Past tense: Ate
- Past participle: Eaten

6. Drink

- Base form: Drink
- Past tense: Drank
- Past participle: Drunk

7. Take

- Base form: Take
- Past tense: Took
- Past participle: Taken

8. Drive

- Base form: Drive
- Past tense: Drove
- Past participle: Driven

9. Speak

- Base form: Speak
- Past tense: Spoke
- Past participle: Spoken

10. Write

- Base form: Write
- Past tense: Wrote
- Past participle: Written

These are just a few examples of irregular verbs in English. It's important to note that irregular verbs do not follow a consistent pattern, so they need to be memorized individually. Regular verbs, on the other hand, follow a predictable pattern when conjugated in different tenses.

5-7

Teaching verb tenses effectively

Teaching verb tenses effectively is crucial for helping students communicate accurately and fluently in English. Here are some strategies and tips for teaching verb tenses effectively:

1. **Start with the Basics:** Begin by teaching the basic tenses, such as the simple present, simple past, and simple future. Ensure that students have a solid grasp of these fundamental tenses before moving on to more complex ones.

2. **Use Clear Examples:** Provide clear and relatable examples for each tense. Use real-life scenarios and context to help students understand when and how to use each tense. Visual aids, such as timelines or diagrams, can also be helpful.

3. **Practice with Regular and Irregular Verbs:** Emphasize the difference between regular and irregular verbs when teaching past tenses. Have students practice conjugating both types of verbs to reinforce the rules.

4. **Interactive Activities:** Engage students in interactive activities that require them to use different tenses in conversation or written exercises. Role-playing, storytelling, and group discussions are effective ways to practice verb tenses in context.

5. **Tense-specific Exercises:** Design exercises that specifically target each tense. For example, for the present continuous tense, have students describe what they are doing right now. For the past perfect, ask them to narrate events in a story.

6. **Progressive Complexity:** Introduce tenses gradually, starting with the most basic and progressing to more advanced ones. This helps students build a strong foundation before tackling complex tenses like the present perfect continuous.

7. **Compare and Contrast:** Encourage students to compare and contrast tenses that are commonly confused, such as present perfect vs. simple past. Highlight the key differences in usage and time frame.

8. **Error Analysis:** Review common errors students make when using different tenses. Discuss why these errors occur and provide guidance on how to correct them.

9. **Regular Review:** Regularly review previously learned tenses to reinforce retention. Use quizzes or review games to make the process engaging.

10. **Authentic Materials:** Incorporate authentic materials like songs, movie clips, news articles, and short stories that use different tenses. This exposes students to real-world usage and makes learning more interesting.

11. **Individualized Feedback:** Provide individualized feedback on students' written and spoken work, focusing on their use of verb tenses. This helps them understand their strengths and areas for improvement.

12. **Use Technology:** Incorporate online resources, grammar-checking tools, and language- learning apps that offer exercises and explanations for various tenses.

13. **Encourage Self-study:** Encourage students to practice verb tenses independently through exercises in

grammar workbooks or online resources. Assign homework that reinforces what was learned in class.

14. **Contextual Learning:** Teach tenses in the context of real-life situations and topics that interest your students. This makes learning more relevant and engaging.

15. **Patience and Positive Reinforcement:** Understand that mastering verb tenses can be challenging, especially for non-native speakers. Be patient, provide positive reinforcement, and create a supportive learning environment.

Remember that teaching verb tenses effectively requires a combination of structured lessons, practice, and ongoing reinforcement. Adapt your teaching methods to the needs and proficiency levels of your students, and don't rush through the material. Building a strong foundation in verb tenses is essential for effective English communication.

Chapter 6

Articles and Determiners

6-1

Articles (a, an, the)

Certainly! Articles are an important part of English grammar, and they help specify and identify nouns (people, places, things, or ideas) in sentences. In English, there are three main articles: "a," "an," and "the." Let's explore each of them in detail:

1. Indefinite Articles ("a" and "an"):
    - "A" is used before words that start with a consonant sound. For example:
        - *I saw a dog in the park.*
        - *She is a teacher.*
    - "An" is used before words that start with a vowel sound. For example:
        - *I saw an owl in the tree.*
        - *She is an excellent student.*
        Note that it's the sound that matters, not necessarily the letter itself. For instance, "hour" starts with the letter 'h,' a consonant, but it has a vowel sound, so you'd say, "I waited for **an** hour."

2. **Definite Article ("the"):**
    - "The" is used when you are referring to a specific noun that is already known or has been mentioned earlier in the conversation. It is used for both singular and plural nouns. For example:
        - *I saw the dog that chased the cat yesterday.*
        - *She is the best student in the class.*

        "The" implies that the speaker and the listener or reader both know which specific thing or things they are talking about.

3. **Zero Article:**

    Sometimes, no article is needed before a noun. This is known as the "zero article." It is used in the following situations:
    - **General Statements:** When you are talking about something in a general or abstract sense, you typically omit the article.
        - *Dogs are loyal animals.*
        - *Happiness is important.*
    - **Plural Nouns Used Generically:** When referring to plural nouns in a general or generic sense, you often omit the article.
        - *Cats are independent animals.*
        - *Doctors help people.*
    - **Uncountable Nouns:** Many uncountable nouns (e.g., water, air, love) do not take an article unless you are specifying a particular instance.
        - *I need water.*
        - *She has a glass of wine.*

4. Special Cases:
   - **Proper Nouns:** Names of specific people, places, or things typically do not require an article.
     - *I visited Paris last summer.*
     - *John is my friend.*
   - **Noun Plurals:** In general, plurals do not require an article when used generically.
     - *Apples are delicious.*
     - *Birds sing in the morning.*
   - **Meals and Times of the Day:** Often, we don't use articles before meals or times of the day.
     - *We had breakfast together.*
     - *He works at night.*

In summary, articles (a, an, the) play a crucial role in English grammar by specifying and clarifying which nouns you are referring to. Using the correct article helps convey the intended meaning and context in your sentences, whether you're talking about something specific or making general statements. Mastering the use of articles can greatly improve the clarity and accuracy of your English communication.

6-2

Demonstratives

Demonstratives are a crucial part of English grammar that help speakers and writers indicate and specify objects or people in relation to themselves and others. Demonstratives are typically used to answer questions like "Which one?" or "Whose is this?" They provide important context and clarity in communication. In English, there are four main demonstratives: "this," "these," "that," and "those." Let's delve into these demonstratives and how they function in the language:

1. This:
    - **Singular:** "This" is used to refer to a singular item or person that is near the speaker. It suggests proximity. For example, "This book is interesting."
    - **Abstract:** It can also be used in an abstract sense to refer to an idea or concept mentioned earlier. For example, "This is what I meant."

2. These:

- **Plural:** "These" is the plural form of "this" and is used to refer to multiple items or people that are near the speaker. For example, "These apples are delicious."
- **Abstract:** Similar to "this," "these" can be used in an abstract sense when referring to multiple ideas or concepts. For example, "These are the solutions to our problems."

3. **That:**
   - **Singular:** "That" is used to refer to a singular item or person that is distant from the speaker. It suggests remoteness. For example, "That car is expensive."
   - **Abstract:** Like "this," "that" can also be used abstractly to refer to an idea or concept mentioned earlier. For example, "That's what I was talking about."

4. **Those:**
   - **Plural:** "Those" is the plural form of "that" and is used to refer to multiple items or people that are distant from the speaker. For example, "Those flowers in the garden are beautiful."
   - **Abstract:** "Those" can be used in an abstract sense when referring to multiple ideas or concepts. For example, "Those are the issues we need to address."

Key Points to Remember:

- Demonstratives are often accompanied by nouns to specify which item or person they are referring to. For example, "This book" or "Those students."
- Demonstratives can be used in both formal and informal language.
- Demonstratives can be used in various tenses. For instance, "That was my first car" (past), "This is my favorite song" (present), and "These will be your responsibilities" (future).
- Demonstratives can also be used in combination with prepositions. For example, "I am looking at that painting" (with the preposition "at").
- Demonstratives can help establish a sense of order, importance, or priority. For example, "First, I'll discuss this issue, and then I'll address that one."
- When referring to objects or people whose identity is clear from the context, you can use demonstratives alone. For example, if you and your friend are looking at a group of cars, you can simply say, "I like this one," pointing to the specific car you are talking about.

In summary, demonstratives are essential linguistic tools that allow us to pinpoint and specify objects, people, or ideas in relation to our position or the context of the conversation. Mastering the correct usage of demonstratives is crucial for effective communication in English and can significantly enhance the clarity and precision of your language.

6-3

Quantifiers

English quantifiers are words or phrases that provide information about the quantity or amount of a noun in a sentence. They help to specify whether a noun is being referred to in a general or specific sense, and they can convey a wide range of meanings related to quantity, frequency, and degree. Understanding quantifiers is essential for clear and precise communication in English. In this comprehensive explanation, we will explore the types of quantifiers, their usage, and examples.

Types of Quantifiers:

1. **Definite Numerals:** These quantifiers specify an exact quantity or number and leave no room for ambiguity. Common examples include:
    - one, two, three, four, etc.
    - a dozen, a hundred, a thousand, etc.
    - a million, a billion, etc.

    Example: There are **three** apples on the table.

2. **Indefinite Numerals:** These quantifiers give a general idea of quantity without specifying an exact number. Common examples include:
   - some
   - several
   - many
   - few
   - a few
   - a couple of
   - numerous

   Examples:
   - I have **some** books to read.
   - There are **several** options to choose from.
   - How **many** people attended the meeting?

3. **Universal Quantifiers:** These quantifiers express the idea of "all" or "every." Common examples include:
   - all
   - every
   - each
   - both
   - neither

   Examples:
   - **All** students must complete the assignment.
   - **Every** child loves ice cream.

4. **Existential Quantifiers:** These quantifiers indicate the existence of something or someone. Common examples include:
   - some
   - any

- no

Examples:
- I need to buy **some** groceries.
- Have you seen **any** good movies lately?
- There are **no** cookies left.

5. **Fractional Quantifiers:** These quantifiers express a portion or fraction of a whole. Common examples include:
   - half
   - a quarter
   - one-third
   - three-quarters

   Examples:
   - I ate **half** of the pizza.
   - She drank **a quarter** of the juice.

Usage of Quantifiers:

1. **Countable Nouns:** Quantifiers are often used with countable nouns, which are nouns that can be counted as individual units (e.g., apples, books, students).
   - **Some** apples
   - **Two** books
   - **Many** students

2. **Uncountable Nouns:** Quantifiers can also be used with uncountable nouns, which represent things that cannot be counted as distinct units (e.g., water, information, money).
   - **Some** water
   - **A lot of** information

- **Little** money

Notes:

- Quantifiers can be used in both affirmative and negative sentences, as well as questions.
- The choice of quantifier depends on the context and the intended meaning of the sentence.
- Some quantifiers, like "all," "every," and "both," can only be used with countable nouns.
- Others, like "some," "any," and "much," are typically used with uncountable nouns.

Examples:

1. Affirmative sentence with countable noun:
    - **Several** students passed the
2. Negative sentence with countable noun:
    - There were **no** cookies
3. Affirmative sentence with uncountable noun:
    - She has **a lot of**
4. Negative sentence with uncountable noun:
    - There is **not much** time left.
5. Question:
    - **How many** people are attending the conference?

In conclusion, quantifiers are essential elements in English grammar that help convey the quantity, frequency, or degree of nouns in sentences. Using the appropriate quantifier is crucial for effective communication, and understanding their various types and usages is fundamental for mastering the English language.

6-4

Possessive determiners

Possessive determiners, also known as possessive adjectives, are a type of grammatical element used in the English language to indicate possession or ownership. They are called "determiners" because they determine or specify to whom a particular noun belongs. Possessive determiners help clarify the relationship between the owner and the thing that is owned. In English, there are seven primary possessive determiners: "my," "your," "his," "her," "its," "our," and "their."

Here is a comprehensive explanation of possessive determiners, including their usage, forms, and examples:

1. Forms of Possessive Determiners:
    - My: Indicates possession by the speaker or the first person singular. For example, "This is my book."
    - Your: Indicates possession by the person or people being addressed or the second person singular or plural. For example, "Is this your car?"

- **His:** Indicates possession by a male person or thing, which is the third person singular. For example, "That is **his** hat."
- **Her:** Indicates possession by a female person or thing, which is also the third person singular. For example, "I like **her** dress."
- **Its:** Indicates possession by an animal or inanimate object, which is the third person singular. For example, "The cat is licking **its** paw."
- **Our:** Indicates possession by a group to which the speaker belongs, which is the first person plural. For example, "We all contributed to **our** project."
- **Their:** Indicates possession by a group of people or things, which is the third person plural. For example, "Those are **their** bikes."

2. Usage of Possessive Determiners:
    - **Ownership:** Possessive determiners are primarily used to show ownership or possession of something. They answer the question "Whose?" For example, "Whose pen is this?" - "It's **my** pen."
    - **Attribution:** Possessive determiners can also be used to attribute qualities or characteristics to a particular person or thing. For example, "That's **his** genius idea."
    - **Relationships:** They can indicate relationships between people or things. For instance, "She's **my** sister," or "This is **our** house."
    - **Emphasis:** Possessive determiners can be used for emphasis or to stress the ownership aspect

of a noun. For example, "This is my computer, not yours."

3. Contractions:
   In casual speech and writing, possessive determiners are often contracted with the verb "to be." Here are some common contractions:
   - I am → I'm
   - You are → You're
   - He is → He's
   - She is → She's
   - It is → It's
   - We are → We're
   - They are → They're
     For example, "I'm excited about my vacation."

4. Agreement with Nouns:
   Possessive determiners agree in gender and number with the noun they modify. This means that the form of the determiner may change based on whether the noun is singular or plural and whether it refers to a male, female, or inanimate object. For example:
   - Singular male: **His** book
   - Singular female: **Her** book
   - Singular inanimate: **Its** cover
   - Plural: **Their** books

5. Possessive Pronouns vs. Possessive Determiners:
   It's important to distinguish between possessive determiners and possessive pronouns. While possessive determiners come before nouns and indicate owner-

ship, possessive pronouns replace nouns and indicate ownership without needing a noun. For example:
- **Possessive Determiner:** This is my car. (The determiner "my" modifies the noun "car.")
- **Possessive Pronoun:** This car is mine. (The pronoun "mine" replaces the noun and indicates ownership.)

In summary, possessive determiners are essential elements of English grammar used to indicate ownership or possession. They agree with the gender and number of the nouns they modify and are employed to specify the owner of an object, emphasize ownership, or show relationships between people or things. Understanding how to use possessive determiners correctly is fundamental to clear and effective communication in English.

Chapter 7

Adjectives and Adverbs

7-1

Using Adjectives

Adjectives are an essential part of English grammar. They are words that describe or modify nouns (people, places, things, or ideas) by providing more information about their qualities, characteristics, or attributes. Here are some key points to keep in mind when using adjectives in English:

1. **Placement:** Adjectives typically come before the noun they modify. For example:
    - A **red** car
    - **Beautiful** flowers
    - An **interesting** book

2. **Order:** When using multiple adjectives to describe a single noun, there is a specific order in which they should appear. This order is known as the "OSASCOMP" rule:
    - Opinion (e.g., beautiful)
    - Size (e.g., small)
    - Age (e.g., old)
    - Shape (e.g., round)
    - Color (e.g., blue)
    - Origin (e.g., Italian)

- Material (e.g., wooden)
- Purpose (e.g., cooking)
  For example: "She wore a **beautiful small old round blue Italian wooden cooking** spoon."

3. **Comparative and Superlative Forms:** Adjectives can have comparative and superlative forms to compare two or more things.
    - Comparative: Used to compare two things. Typically formed by adding "-er" to the adjective or using "more" before it. For example: "Taller," "more interesting."
    - Superlative: Used to compare three or more things. Typically formed by adding "- est" to the adjective or using "most" before it. For example: "Tallest," "most interesting."

4. **Using Adverbs:** You can modify adjectives with adverbs to provide additional information about the adjective. For example:
    - She is **extremely** talented.
    - The movie was **very** entertaining.

5. **Predicative vs. Attributive Adjectives:** Adjectives can be used either attributively (before the noun) or predicatively (after a linking verb like "is," "seems," "becomes," etc.). For example:
    - **Attributive:** The **blue** sky.
    - **Predicative:** The sky **is blue**.

6. **Articles:** Adjectives often appear with articles (a, an, the) when modifying nouns. For example:
    - **A** big house
    - **The** happy child

7. **Demonstrative Adjectives:** Words like "this," "that," "these," and "those" can also function as adjectives when used to point out specific nouns. For example:
    - I like **this** book.
    - Please give me **those** cookies.

8. **Possessive Adjectives:** Words like "my," "your," "his," "her," "its," "our," and "their" indicate ownership or possession and are used to modify nouns. For example:
    - **My** cat is playful.
    - **Their** car is parked outside.

9. **Limiting Adjectives:** Words like "some," "many," "few," and "several" are used to specify the quantity or limit of nouns. For example:
    - I have **some** apples.
    - **Many** people attended the event.

Remember that the choice of adjectives can greatly impact the imagery and clarity of your writing or speech, so choose them carefully to convey your intended message effectively.

7-2

Using Adverbs

Adverbs are a vital part of the English language that add depth and specificity to verbs, adjectives, other adverbs, or entire sentences. They provide information about how, when, where, or to what degree an action or adjective occurs. Here are some common ways to use adverbs in English:

1. Modifying Verbs:
    - *He ran quickly.*
    - *She sings beautifully.*
    - *They spoke softly.*

2. Modifying Adjectives:
    - *The car is very fast.*
    - *She is extremely talented.*
    - *The movie was quite boring.*

3. Modifying Other Adverbs:
    - *He works exceptionally quickly.*
    - *She types incredibly accurately.*
    - *They completed the task rather easily.*

4. **Modifying Entire Sentences** (often at the beginning or end):
    - *Certainly, I will help you.*
    - *Sadly, he couldn't make it.*
    - *She finished the race first, undoubtedly.*

5. **Frequency Adverbs** (indicate how often something happens):
    - *He always arrives early.*
    - *She rarely complains.*
    - *They occasionally go to the beach.*

6. **Adverbs of Time** (indicate when something happens):
    - *They will meet tomorrow.*
    - *He arrived late.*
    - *She studies every day.*

7. **Adverbs of Place** (indicate where something happens):
    - *They looked everywhere for the keys.*
    - *She left her bag here.*
    - *He found it there.*

8. **Adverbs of Manner** (indicate how something is done):
    - *He solved the problem methodically.*
    - *She danced gracefully.*
    - *They argued fiercely.*

9. **Adverbs of Degree** (indicate the extent or intensity of an action or adjective):
    - *She is quite tall.*
    - *He is extremely excited.*
    - *They are somewhat disappointed.*

10. **Adverbs of Certainty** (indicate the level of certainty or probability):
    - *I will probably attend the party.*
    - *They are definitely coming.*
    - *She might be late.*

11. **Adverbs of Comparison** (used to compare two or more things):
    - *She sings better than he does.*
    - *He runs faster than his brother.*
    - *They work more efficiently as a team.*

12. **Adverbs in Questions** (used to inquire about specific details):
    - *Why did you do that?*
    - *How are you feeling?*
    - *When will they arrive?*

Remember that the placement of adverbs can vary in a sentence, and their position can affect the meaning or emphasis. Generally, adverbs are placed before the verb they modify, but they can also appear at the beginning or end of a sentence or clause for emphasis. Adverbs of frequency often come before the main verb.

Using adverbs effectively can make your writing and speech more descriptive and precise, enhancing your communication in English.

7-3

Degrees of Comparison

Degrees of comparison in English grammar refer to the different forms of adjectives and adverbs that are used to compare and contrast the qualities of nouns and verbs. There are three degrees of comparison: positive, comparative, and superlative. These degrees allow us to express the degree or extent to which something possesses a certain quality.

1. Positive Degree:
    - The positive degree is the simplest form of an adjective or adverb, and it is used to describe a quality without making any comparison. It merely states a fact or quality about something.
    - Example with adjectives: "She is a good student."
    - Example with adverbs: "He sings well."

2. Comparative Degree:
    - The comparative degree is used to compare two or more things or actions, indicating which one

has a higher or lower degree of a particular quality than the other(s).
- For most one-syllable adjectives, you add "-er" to the adjective to form the comparative degree.
  - Example: "She is taller than her brother."
- For most adjectives with two or more syllables, you use "more" or "less" before the adjective to form the comparative degree.
  - Example: "He is more intelligent than his classmates."
- For adverbs, you typically add "more" or "less" before the adverb.
  - Example: "She dances more gracefully than he does."

3. **Superlative Degree:**
   - The superlative degree is used to compare three or more things or actions and indicates which one has the highest or lowest degree of a particular quality.
   - For most one-syllable adjectives, you add "-est" to the adjective to form the superlative degree.
     - Example: "She is the tallest student in her class."
   - For most adjectives with two or more syllables, you use "most" or "least" before the adjective to form the superlative degree.
     - Example: "He is the most talented musician in the band."

- For adverbs, you typically add "most" or "least" before the adverb.
  - Example: "She sings most beautifully of all."

It's important to note that there are some irregular adjectives and adverbs that don't follow these rules, and their comparative and superlative forms need to be memorized. For example:

- Good -> Better (comparative) -> Best (superlative)
- Bad -> Worse (comparative) -> Worst (superlative)
  When comparing two things, you can use "than" after the comparative form. For superlatives, "the" is commonly used before the superlative form to specify which thing or person is the most or least in a group.
  Examples:
- "She is smarter than her sister."
- "This is the most interesting book I've ever read."
- "He swims less gracefully than she does."

In summary, degrees of comparison are essential in English grammar to express the level of a quality possessed by a noun or verb in relation to other nouns or verbs. Adjectives and adverbs are modified to indicate whether something is equal, greater, or lesser in quality, making it easier to compare and describe various aspects of the world around us.

7-4

Common Adjective and Adverb Errors

Common adjective and adverb errors in English can occur due to various reasons, including confusion about their usage or placement in a sentence. Here are some common errors to watch out for:

1. Confusing Adjectives and Adverbs:
    - Adjectives describe nouns, while adverbs modify verbs, adjectives, or other adverbs. A common mistake is using an adjective when an adverb is needed, or vice versa.
    Incorrect: She sings beautiful.
    Correct: She sings beautifully.

2. Double Negatives:
    - Using double negatives can lead to confusion because they cancel each other out, making the sentence positive when you intend it to be negative.
    Incorrect: I don't want no more cake.
    Correct: I don't want any more cake.

3. Misplacing Adverbs:
    - Adverbs should be placed as close as possible to the verb or adjective they are modifying. Misplaced adverbs can change the intended meaning of a sentence.
    Incorrect: He almost passed all his exams.
    Correct: He passed almost all his exams.

4. Comparative and Superlative Forms:
    - Adjectives and adverbs have comparative (comparing two things) and superlative (comparing more than two things) forms. It's important to use them correctly.
    Incorrect: She is the most tallest girl in the class.
    Correct: She is the tallest girl in the class.

5. Using "Good" and "Well" Incorrectly:
    - "Good" is an adjective, while "well" is an adverb. People often use "good" when they should use "well" to describe an action.
    Incorrect: She plays the piano good.
    Correct: She plays the piano well.

6. Redundancy with Adverbs:
    - Sometimes, people use adverbs that are unnecessary because the meaning is already clear from the verb.
    Incorrect: He ran quickly.
    Correct: He ran.

7. Overusing Adverbs:
    - Overusing adverbs can make your writing or speech sound weak or cluttered. Use them sparingly and focus on strong verbs and adjectives instead.
    Weak: She smiled really happily.
    Strong: She beamed.

8. Incorrectly Formed Adjective Clauses:
    - Adjective clauses provide additional information about a noun, and they need to be introduced by words like "who," "which," or "that."
    Incorrect: The car she bought is expensive.
    Correct: The car that she bought is expensive.

9. Confusing "Farther" and "Further":
    - "Farther" is used for physical distance, while "further" is used for metaphorical or abstract distance.
    Incorrect: We need to discuss this farther.
    Correct: We need to discuss this further.

10. Inconsistent Comparisons:
    - When making comparisons, be consistent in your choice of words and structures.

    Incorrect: She is more friendly than Susan, but Carol is the friendliest.
    Correct: She is friendlier than Susan, but Carol is the friendliest.

To improve your understanding of adjectives and adverbs, it's essential to practice and pay attention to their usage in context. Reading and writing regularly can help you avoid these common errors.

Chapter 8

Pronouns and Agreement

8-1

Personal Pronouns

Personal pronouns are words used to replace or refer to specific individuals or groups of individuals in a sentence. They play a crucial role in language by helping us avoid repetitive or cumbersome language. Personal pronouns can be divided into several categories based on the grammatical person, number, and gender of the individuals they refer to. Here are the main categories of personal pronouns:

- **First Person Pronouns**: These pronouns refer to the speaker or
    - Singular: I (for the speaker)
    - Plural: We (for the speaker and others)

Example sentences:

- I am going to the store.
- We are going to the store.

- **Second Person Pronouns**: These pronouns refer to the person or people being spoken
    - Singular: You
    - Plural: You (used for both singular and plural)

Example sentences:

- You should come with us.
- Are you all coming to the party?

- **Third Person Pronouns**: These pronouns refer to individuals or groups of individuals who are not the speaker or the person being spoken to. They can be further divided based on
    - Singular Masculine: He
    - Singular Feminine: She
    - Singular Neuter (for objects, animals, or things): It
    - Plural: They (used for all genders and groups)

Example sentences:

- He is a doctor.
- She is going to the bank.
- It is raining outside.
- They are playing in the yard.

It's important to note that English pronouns do not change based on formal or informal address, unlike some other languages. "You" is used both for formal and informal situations.

8-2

Demonstrative Pronouns

Demonstrative pronouns are a type of pronoun used to indicate or point to specific people, things, or ideas in a sentence. They help provide clarity and context by specifying whether something is near or far in relation to the speaker or the listener. In English, there are four main demonstrative pronouns: "this," "that," "these," and "those."

1. **This:** "This" is used to indicate a singular item or idea that is close to the speaker. For example, "This book is interesting."

2. **That:** "That" is used to indicate a singular item or idea that is farther away from the speaker. For example, "That car over there is mine."

3. **These:** "These" is the plural form of "this," and it is used to indicate multiple items or ideas that are

close to the speaker. For example, "These cookies are delicious."

4. **Those:** "Those" is the plural form of "that," and it is used to indicate multiple items or ideas that are farther away from the speaker. For example, "Those mountains in the distance are beautiful."

Demonstrative pronouns can be used to replace nouns in a sentence to avoid repetition and make the text more concise. They are commonly used to clarify which specific items or concepts are being referred to in a conversation or written text.

8-3

Indefinite Pronouns

Indefinite pronouns are pronouns that do not refer to any specific person, thing, or amount. Instead, they refer to non-specific people, things, or quantities in a more general or vague way. Indefinite pronouns are commonly used in English to avoid repetition and to make sentences less specific. Here are some common examples of indefinite pronouns:

1. Singular Indefinite Pronouns:
    - **Anyone:** Refers to any person.
    - **Someone:** Refers to a person, but not a specific one.
    - **No one/Nobody:** Refers to no person.
    - **Everyone:** Refers to all people.

2. Plural Indefinite Pronouns:
    - **Some:** Refers to an unspecified number or quantity of something.
    - **Many:** Refers to a large but unspecified number.
    - **Few:** Refers to a small number.
    - **Several:** Refers to more than two but not many.

- **All:** Refers to the whole or complete group.

3. **Singular or Plural Indefinite Pronouns:**
    - **All:** Can refer to a singular or plural noun depending on the context.
    - **None:** Can also refer to a singular or plural noun depending on the context.
    - **Any:** Can refer to a singular or plural noun depending on the context.
    - **Some:** Can also refer to a singular or plural noun depending on the context.

4. **Other Indefinite Pronouns:**
    - **Something:** Refers to an unspecified thing.
    - **Nothing:** Refers to no thing.
    - **Everything:** Refers to all things.
    - **Anything:** Refers to any thing.
    - **Everywhere:** Refers to all places.
    - **Nowhere:** Refers to no place.
    - **Somewhere:** Refers to an unspecified place.
    - **Anywhere:** Refers to any place.

Indefinite pronouns are versatile and can be used in various contexts, such as when you want to make general statements, ask questions, or convey uncertainty. Keep in mind that the choice of indefinite pronoun depends on the context and the noun it replaces or refers to in a sentence.

Here are some common indefinite pronouns and their agreement rules:

1. **Singular Indefinite Pronouns:**

- Anyone: Anyone can join the club.
- Someone: Someone is at the door.
- Nobody: Nobody wants to be alone.
- Anything: Anything is possible.

2. Plural Indefinite Pronouns:
    - All: All are welcome to the party.
    - Some: Some were happy with the decision.
    - Many: Many have already left.
    - Few: Few attended the meeting.
3. Singular or Plural Indefinite Pronouns:
    - Both: Both are correct.
    - Neither: Neither is true.
    - Either: Either option is fine.
    - None: None of the books are mine.
4. Gender-Neutral Indefinite Pronouns:
    - Singular: They/Them/Their
        - Anyone can use their preferred pronouns.
    - Plural: They/Them/Their
        - They are my friends, and I respect their choices.
    - Singular: Singular "they" is also used as a gender-neutral singular pronoun when the gender of the person is unknown or irrelevant.
        - If someone calls, tell them I'll call them back.

Agreement rules for indefinite pronouns:

- Singular indefinite pronouns (e.g., anyone, someone, nobody) take singular verbs and adjectives. For example, "Nobody is here."
- Plural indefinite pronouns (e.g., all, some, many) take plural verbs and adjectives. For example, "All are welcome."

- "Both," "neither," "either," and "none" can take either singular or plural verbs and adjectives depending on the context.
- Gender-neutral pronouns like "they/them" are used when referring to individuals who may not identify as strictly male or female.

It's important to pay attention to the context and agreement rules when using indefinite pronouns to ensure that your sentences are grammatically correct and convey the intended meaning.

8-4

Reflexive Pronouns

Reflexive pronouns are a type of pronoun used to refer back to the subject of a sentence or clause. They indicate that the action of the verb is being performed by the subject on itself. Reflexive pronouns are essential in many languages, including English, to convey actions of self or actions directed back toward the subject. In English, reflexive pronouns are formed by adding "-self" (singular) or "-selves" (plural) to certain personal pronouns. Here are the reflexive pronouns in English:

Singular:

- Myself
- Yourself
- Himself
- Herself
- Itself (used for animals or inanimate objects)
- Oneself (used less frequently) Plural:
- Ourselves
- Yourselves
- Themselves

Here are some examples of how reflexive pronouns are used in sentences:

1. I cut myself while cooking dinner. (The reflexive pronoun "myself" refers back to the subject "I," indicating that I performed the action of cutting on myself.)
2. She taught herself how to play the piano. (The reflexive pronoun "herself" refers back to the subject "She," indicating that she learned to play the piano on her own.)
3. They blamed themselves for the mistake. (The reflexive pronoun "themselves" refers back to the subject "They," indicating that they were responsible for the mistake.)
4. We need to take care of ourselves. (The reflexive pronoun "ourselves" refers back to the subject "We," emphasizing the need for self-care.)
5. You should be proud of yourselves for your hard work. (The reflexive pronoun "yourselves" refers back to the subject "You," acknowledging the collective effort.)

Reflexive pronouns are also used in various other contexts, such as for emphasis, to show reciprocity, or to indicate that an action is being done willingly. Understanding when and how to use reflexive pronouns is an important aspect of English grammar.

8-5

Pronoun-Antecedent Agreement

Pronoun-antecedent agreement is a grammatical rule that states that a pronoun must agree in number, person, and gender with its antecedent in a sentence. An antecedent is the word or phrase to which a pronoun refers. Here are some key points to remember about pronoun-antecedent agreement:

1. Number Agreement:
    - Singular antecedents should be paired with singular pronouns. For example, "The boy (singular) is playing with his (singular) toy."
    - Plural antecedents should be paired with plural pronouns. For example, "The children (plural) are playing with their (plural) toys."

2. Person Agreement:
    - First-person pronouns (I, me, we, us) should match with first-person antecedents.

- Second-person pronouns (you, your) should match with second-person antecedents.
- Third-person pronouns (he, him, she, her, it, they, them) should match with third- person antecedents.

3. **Gender Agreement:**
   - Gender-specific pronouns should match the gender of the antecedent. For example, "She (female) is a doctor. He (male) is an engineer."
   - When the gender of the antecedent is unknown or the antecedent is a group of people of mixed genders, you can use gender-neutral pronouns like "they" or "them." For example, "The team is doing well; they are working hard."

4. **Agreement with Indefinite Pronouns:**
   - Some indefinite pronouns, like "everyone," "someone," and "each," are singular and should be paired with singular pronouns. For example, "Everyone should bring his or her own lunch."
   - Other indefinite pronouns, like "both," "few," and "several," are plural and should be paired with plural pronouns. For example, "Both of the students completed their assignments."

5. **Agreement with Collective Nouns:**

- Collective nouns, which refer to a group of people or things, can be treated as singular or plural depending on the context. For example, "The team is celebrating its victory" (singular) and "The team are arguing among themselves" (plural).

Remember that maintaining pronoun-antecedent agreement is important for clarity and effective communication in writing. Failing to follow these agreement rules can lead to confusion and grammatical errors.

8-6

Avoiding Pronoun Ambiguity

Avoiding pronoun ambiguity is important in writing to ensure that your readers can clearly understand which nouns the pronouns refer to. Pronoun ambiguity can lead to confusion and a breakdown in communication. Here are some tips to help you avoid pronoun ambiguity:

1. **Use Specific Nouns**: Whenever possible, use specific nouns instead of pronouns. This not only eliminates ambiguity but also makes your writing more precise. For example, instead of writing, "She told him that she would call later," you can write, "Maria told John that she would call later."

2. **Repeat Nouns**: It's okay to repeat nouns to avoid ambiguity. While repeating nouns may make your writing seem a bit repetitive, it's better than causing confusion. For example, instead of writing, "The cat chased its tail. It was spinning rapidly," you can write, "The cat chased its tail. The tail was spinning rapidly."

3. **Antecedent Clarity**: Make sure the antecedent (the noun to which the pronoun refers) is clear and unambiguous. Readers should be able to easily identify what the pronoun is replacing. For example, "When she saw the dog, it was barking loudly" is ambiguous because it's unclear whether "it" refers to the woman or the dog.

4. **Use Descriptive Phrases**: If there's a risk of confusion, use descriptive phrases or clauses to clarify the antecedent. For example, instead of writing, "He gave the book to his friend, which was a bestseller," you can write, "He gave the book, which was a bestseller, to his friend."

5. **Switch Pronouns or Reword**: Sometimes, simply switching the pronoun or rephrasing the sentence can eliminate ambiguity. For example, instead of writing, "He said he liked the movie, but she didn't," you can write, "He said he liked the movie, but she disagreed."

6. **Check for Multiple Antecedents**: Be cautious when multiple nouns could be the antecedent for a pronoun in the same sentence. If there's potential for confusion, consider rewording the sentence or using specific nouns.

7. **Be Mindful of Gender Pronouns**: Pay attention to gender pronouns (he/she) and use them appropriately based on the gender of the antecedent. If gender is unknown or irrelevant, you can use gender-neutral pronouns like "they" or rephrase the sentence to avoid gender-specific pronouns.

8. **Proofread Carefully**: After you've written your text, proofread it carefully to identify and correct any instances of pronoun ambiguity. Reading your writing aloud can help you catch many of these issues.

9. **Get Feedback**: If you're unsure about whether your writing contains pronoun ambiguity, ask someone else to read it and provide feedback. Fresh eyes can often spot issues that you might have missed.

By following these guidelines, you can improve the clarity of your writing and ensure that your readers understand the relationships between pronouns and their antecedents.

Chapter 9

Prepositions and Phrasal Verbs

9-1

Common Prepositions

Prepositions are words that show the relationship between different elements in a sentence. They are commonly used to indicate location, time, direction, and other relationships between nouns, pronouns, and other words in a sentence. Here is a list of common prepositions in English:

1. **In**: Used to indicate location inside a place or a period of time.
    - The book is **in** the bag.
    - She was born **in** June.

2. **On**: Used to indicate location on a surface or a specific day.
    - The cat is **on** the table.
    - My birthday is **on** Friday.

3. **At**: Used to indicate a specific point or location.
    - I am **at** the park.

- The meeting is **at** 3 o'clock.

4. **By**: Used to indicate nearness or a method of transportation.
    - I will pick you up **by** car.
    - The bookshelf is **by** the window.

5. **For**: Used to indicate purpose, duration, or benefit.
    - She bought a gift **for** her friend.
    - I'll be away **for** a week.

6. **With**: Used to indicate accompaniment or association.
    - I went to the party **with** my friends.
    - He painted the picture **with** watercolors.

7. **To**: Used to indicate movement or direction.
    - I am going **to** the store.
    - She gave the gift **to** him.

8. **From**: Used to indicate the starting point of something.
    - The train departs **from** the station.
    - I received a letter **from** my grandmother.

9. **Into**: Used to indicate movement toward the inside or a transformation.
    - He jumped **into** the pool.
    - The caterpillar turned **into** a butterfly.

10. **Over**: Used to indicate movement or position above something.
    - The plane flew **over** the mountains.
    - The cat jumped **over** the fence.

11. **Under**: Used to indicate position below or beneath something.
    - The book is **under** the table.
    - The dog is hiding **under** the bed.

12. **Between**: Used to indicate a relationship involving two or more things.
    - The conversation was **between** John and Mary.
    - The restaurant is **between** the bank and the library.

13. **Among**: Used to indicate a relationship involving more than two things.
    - She shared the cookies **among** her friends.
    - He found the key **among** the clutter.

14. **Through**: Used to indicate movement from one side or end to another.
    - The car drove **through** the tunnel.
    - She walked **through** the forest.

15. **Behind**: Used to indicate position in the back of something.

- The cat is hiding **behind** the couch.
- He's the person **behind** the successful project.

16. **Beside**: Used to indicate position next to or alongside something.
    - The pen is **beside** the notebook.
    - I sat **beside** my sister.

17. **Around**: Used to indicate movement in a circular or surrounding manner.
    - They walked **around** the park.
    - He put his arm **around** her.

18. **Above**: Used to indicate position higher than something.
    - The birds are flying **above** the trees.
    - Hang the picture **above** the fireplace.

19. **Below**: Used to indicate position lower than something.
    - The fish swim **below** the surface.
    - The temperature is **below** freezing.

20. **Beneath**: Used to indicate position directly under something.
    - The treasure is buried **beneath** the tree.
    - The truth lies **beneath** the surface.

These are some of the most common prepositions in English, but there are many more. Prepositions play a crucial role in structuring sentences and conveying precise meaning.

9-2

Prepositional Phrases

A prepositional phrase is a group of words that consists of a preposition, its object, and any modifiers of that object. Prepositional phrases are commonly used in English to provide additional information about nouns, pronouns, verbs, or other parts of a sentence. Here's the basic structure of a prepositional phrase:

1. Preposition: A preposition is a word that shows the relationship between its object and other words in the sentence. Common prepositions include "in," "on," "under," "between," "above," "below," "at," "by," "with," and many more.

2. Object: The object of a preposition is a noun or pronoun that the preposition is referring to or modifying.

3. Modifiers: Prepositional phrases can also include modifiers, which are words that further describe the object

of the preposition. These modifiers can include adjectives, adverbs, and other descriptive words.

Here are some examples of prepositional phrases in sentences:

1. She is sitting in the park.
    - Preposition: "in"
    - Object: "park"

2. The book is on the table.
    - Preposition: "on"
    - Object: "table"

3. I went to the store with my friend.
    - Preposition: "to," "with"
    - Objects: "store," "my friend"

4. The cat slept under the bed quietly.
    - Preposition: "under"
    - Object: "bed"
    - Modifier: "quietly"

Prepositional phrases can be used to provide details about location, time, manner, purpose, and more within a sentence. They are versatile and play an essential role in adding context and specificity to the language.

9-3

Prepositions of Time, Place, and Movement

Prepositions are words that typically show the relationship between nouns or pronouns and other elements in a sentence. Prepositions of time, place, and movement are prepositions that specifically indicate when, where, or how something occurs. Here are examples of prepositions in each of these categories:

Prepositions of Time:

- At: Used for specific points in
    - I have a meeting at 9

- **In:** Used for longer periods of
  - I will go on vacation in

- **On:** Used for days and
  - My birthday is on November

- **For:** Indicates the duration of
  - I studied for two

- **Since:** Shows when something
  - I have known her since

- **Until/To:** Indicates the end of a time
  - The store is open until 10

Prepositions of Place:

- **In:** Used for enclosed spaces or larger
    - She is in the
- I live in New
- **At:** Used for specific points or small
    - He is waiting at the bus
    - They are at the

- **On:** Used for
    - The book is on the
    - The picture is on the

- **Under:** Indicates something is beneath or covered by another
    - The cat is under the

- **Over/Above:** Indicates something is higher than or covering another
    - The plane flew over the

- **Below/Beneath:** Indicates something is lower than another
    - The treasure is buried beneath the

Prepositions of Movement:

- **To:** Indicates the direction of
    - She walked to the

- **From:** Indicates the starting point of
    - He traveled from New York to Los

- **Through:** Indicates movement from one side to the
    - They walked through the

- **Across:** Indicates movement from one side to another, usually over
    - They swam across the

- **Along:** Indicates movement in a line or
  - He walked along the

- **Up/Down:** Indicates vertical
  - She climbed up the
  - He walked down the

Remember that the usage of prepositions can be quite nuanced, and there are exceptions and variations depending on context and dialect. It's essential to practice and become familiar with the specific prepositions used in various situations to use them correctly in your writing and speech.

9-4

Phrasal Verbs: Understanding and Teaching Them

Phrasal verbs can be challenging for learners of English because they consist of a verb combined with one or more particles (usually prepositions or adverbs), and their meanings are often idiomatic. Here are some strategies for understanding and teaching phrasal verbs effectively:

For Learners:

1. **Context is Key:** Encourage learners to pay attention to the context in which phrasal verbs are used. Often, the meaning of a phrasal verb can be deduced from the surrounding words and sentences.
2. **Break Down and Define:** Teach learners to break down phrasal verbs into their component parts. Explain the meaning of the verb and the particle(s) separately, and then discuss how they combine to form a new meaning.
3. **Use Real-Life Examples:** Provide real-life examples of phrasal verbs in context, such as from movies, books,

or news articles. This helps learners see how phrasal verbs are used in everyday communication.
4. **Categorize Phrasal Verbs:** Group phrasal verbs into categories based on their meanings or particles (e.g., phrasal verbs related to travel, emotions, or daily routines). This can make it easier for learners to remember and understand them.
5. **Practice, Practice, Practice:** Give learners plenty of opportunities to practice using phrasal verbs in speaking and writing exercises. This could include role-playing, discussions, or writing prompts.

For Teachers:

1. **Start with Common Phrasal Verbs:** Begin by teaching the most commonly used phrasal verbs as they are more likely to encounter these in everyday conversations and texts.
2. **Visual Aids:** Use visual aids like diagrams or illustrations to help learners visualize the meaning of phrasal verbs. This can be especially helpful for visual learners.
3. **Provide a Context:** Whenever you introduce a new phrasal verb, put it in a sentence or a short paragraph. This helps learners see how it's used in context.
4. **Contrast with Similar Words:** Highlight the differences between phrasal verbs and other words that may have similar meanings. For example, compare "give up" with "quit" to show their nuances.
5. **Encourage Self-Study:** Recommend online resources, dictionaries, or apps that learners can use to explore phrasal verbs independently.
6. **Progressive Learning:** Introduce phrasal verbs gradually, starting with simpler ones and moving on to more

complex or idiomatic ones as learners become more proficient.
7. **Testing and Feedback:** Assess learners' understanding of phrasal verbs through quizzes and assignments. Provide constructive feedback to help them improve.
8. **Speaking and Listening Practice:** Incorporate listening exercises and speaking activities where learners have to use phrasal verbs in natural conversations.
9. **Regular Review:** Include periodic review sessions to reinforce previously learned phrasal verbs and ensure they are not forgotten.
10. **Create a Phrasal Verb Wall:** In your classroom, you can have a "Phrasal Verb Wall" where you and your learners can add new phrasal verbs they encounter. Discuss their meanings and use them in sentences as you add them to the wall.

Teaching and understanding phrasal verbs may take time, but with consistent practice and exposure, learners can become more proficient in using them naturally in their English communication.

Chapter 10

Conjunctions and Connectors

10-1

Coordinating Conjunctions

Coordinating conjunctions are an essential part of English grammar that play a crucial role in connecting words, phrases, clauses, or sentences of equal grammatical importance and structure. These conjunctions are called "coordinating" because they serve to coordinate or join elements of equal rank. In English, there are seven primary coordinating conjunctions, often remembered using the acronym FANBOYS:

1. For
2. And
3. Nor
4. But
5. Or
6. Yet
7. So

Let's delve into a comprehensive explanation of coordinating conjunctions:

1. **Conjunction Types:**
    - Coordinating conjunctions connect elements that are similar in structure, such as words to words, phrases to phrases, or clauses to clauses.
    - They are different from subordinating conjunctions, which connect independent and dependent clauses, and correlative conjunctions, which work in pairs (e.g., either/or, neither/nor).

2. **Usage:**
    - Coordinating conjunctions are used to join elements that have equal grammatical importance. These elements can be words, phrases, or clauses.
    - They help create compound sentences, compound words, and compound phrases.

3. **Functions:**
    - **And:** Used to connect words, phrases, or clauses to show addition or a continuation of ideas.
        - Example: "I like coffee, and I like tea."

    - **But:** Used to contrast two ideas or show a difference.
        - Example: "She is tired, but she wants to finish her work."

    - **Or:** Used to present a choice or alternatives.
        - Example: "You can have pizza or pasta for dinner."

- Nor: Used to present a negative choice or alternatives.
    - Example: "He neither called nor texted me."

- For: Often used to explain a reason or purpose.
    - Example: "I stayed home, for I was feeling unwell."

- Yet: Used to show contrast or opposition, often in a compound sentence.
    - Example: "She is tired, yet she keeps working."

- So: Used to indicate a consequence or result.
    - Example: "It was raining, so we stayed indoors."

4. Punctuation:
    - When a coordinating conjunction is used to connect two independent clauses (complete sentences), it is followed by a comma.
        - Example: "I wanted to go to the movies, but I didn't have enough money."

5. Coordinating Conjunctions and Commas:
    - The acronym FANBOYS is often used to remember coordinating conjunctions. Placing a comma before the coordinating conjunction is a

common rule, but it is not always necessary if the sentences are short and closely related.
- Example with a comma: "I like pizza, and she likes pasta."
- Example without a comma: "I like both pizza and pasta."

6. Creating Complex Structures:
   - Coordinating conjunctions can be used to create more complex sentences by combining multiple elements. For example, you can use them to join three or more items in a list.
     - Example: "I need to buy apples, bananas, and oranges."

7. Parallel Structure:
   - When coordinating conjunctions are used in a list or to connect phrases or clauses, it's important to maintain parallel structure, meaning that the elements being connected should have the same grammatical structure.
     - Example: "She enjoys reading, hiking, and swimming."

In summary, coordinating conjunctions are powerful tools in English grammar that help connect words, phrases, or clauses of equal importance. They facilitate the creation of compound sentences, clarify relationships between ideas, and add variety to your writing style.

Understanding when and how to use coordinating conjunctions is essential for effective communication in English.

10-2

Subordinating Conjunctions

Subordinating conjunctions are a crucial component of the English language, as they play a fundamental role in forming complex sentences. These conjunctions are words or phrases that connect two clauses in a sentence, creating a relationship of dependence or subordination between them. Subordinating conjunctions introduce subordinate clauses, which are also known as dependent clauses, and these clauses cannot stand alone as complete sentences but rely on the main clause (independent clause) to make sense.

Here's a comprehensive explanation of subordinating conjunctions:

1. **Definition and Purpose**: Subordinating conjunctions are words or phrases that join a subordinate clause to a main clause, creating a complex sentence. They establish a relationship between the two clauses, showing how they are connected and making the meaning of the sentence more specific or complex.

2. **Examples of Subordinating Conjunctions:** There are numerous subordinating conjunctions in the English language. Some common examples include:
    - *because*: It indicates a cause-and-effect relationship.
    - *although*: It introduces a contrast or concession.
    - *while*: It signifies concurrent actions or events.
    - *if*: It introduces a condition.
    - *since*: It shows a reason or time relationship.
    - *when*: It indicates a specific time or condition.
    - *unless*: It expresses a condition with a negative consequence.

3. **Placement in a Sentence:** Subordinating conjunctions typically appear at the beginning of the subordinate (dependent) clause. For example:
    - *Because it was raining*, I decided to stay indoors.
    - *Although I was tired*, I stayed up late to finish my work.

4. **Relationships Established by Subordinating Conjunctions:** Subordinating conjunctions help clarify the relationship between the main clause and the subordinate clause. Some common relationships include:

- Cause and Effect: Subordinating conjunctions like "because" and "since" introduce clauses that explain why something happened.
- Contrast or Concession: Words like "although" and "though" introduce clauses that provide a counterpoint to the main clause.
- Time: Conjunctions like "when," "while," and "after" establish temporal relationships between the two clauses.
- Condition: "If," "unless," and "provided that" introduce clauses that express conditions.
- Purpose: "So that" and "in order that" introduce clauses that explain why something is done.

5. **Complex Sentences**: Subordinating conjunctions are essential for constructing complex sentences. In complex sentences, one or more subordinate clauses are combined with one main clause to provide additional information, context, or detail. This complexity allows for more nuanced and informative communication.

6. **Punctuation**: When a subordinate clause begins a sentence, it is usually followed by a comma. However, if the subordinate clause comes after the main clause, no comma is needed. For example:
    - *Before I left, I double-checked everything.*
    - *I double-checked everything before I left.*

In summary, subordinating conjunctions are indispensable tools in English grammar, facilitating the construction of complex and varied sentence structures. They allow writers and speakers to convey a wide range of information and relationships between ideas, making communication richer and more precise. Understanding how to use these conjunctions effectively is crucial for achieving clarity and coherence in your writing or speech.

10-3

Correlative Conjunctions

Correlative conjunctions are pairs of words or phrases that work together to join two equal elements within a sentence. They are used to show the relationship between these elements and help create balanced and parallel structures in your writing. Correlative conjunctions always appear in pairs, and each part of the pair serves a specific purpose in the sentence. Common examples of correlative conjunctions include "both...and," "either...or," "neither...nor," "not only...but also," "whether...or," and "not...but."

Here's a comprehensive explanation of correlative conjunctions:

1. **Pairs of Equal Elements:** Correlative conjunctions are used to connect two items or ideas that are of equal importance within a sentence. This means that the elements being joined should be similar in structure or significance. Correlative conjunctions emphasize the

idea that both elements are related and should be considered together.

2. **Balanced Structure:** One of the primary functions of correlative conjunctions is to create balanced and parallel structures in a sentence. This means that the two elements connected by a correlative conjunction should have the same grammatical structure. For example, if the first element is a noun, the second element should also be a noun.

3. **Examples of Correlative Conjunctions:**
    - "Both...and": This conjunction is used to indicate that two things are true or applicable together. For example, "Both Sarah and John are attending the conference."
    - "Either...or": This conjunction presents a choice between two options. For example, "You can either eat the cake or save it for later."
    - "Neither...nor": This conjunction expresses a negative choice or the absence of both options. For example, "Neither the restaurant nor the movie was enjoyable."
    - "Not only...but also": This conjunction is used to emphasize additional information or options. For example, "She is not only intelligent but also hardworking."
    - "Whether...or": This conjunction introduces alternatives or options. For example, "I don't know whether to go to the beach or stay home."

- "Not...but": This conjunction is used to emphasize the contrast between two ideas. For example, "It's not the destination but the journey that matters."

4. **Maintaining Parallelism:** When using correlative conjunctions, it's essential to maintain parallelism in the sentence. This means that the structure and form of the elements being connected should match. For instance, if you start with a verb in one part of the pair, the other part should also have a verb. This consistency makes your writing clearer and more effective.

5. **Clarification and Emphasis:** Correlative conjunctions can also help clarify relationships between ideas and emphasize certain points within a sentence. They allow writers to make their intentions more explicit and highlight specific aspects of the information being presented.

6. **Usage in Complex Sentences:** Correlative conjunctions can be used in both simple and complex sentences. When used in complex sentences, they help create subordinating clauses that add depth and complexity to your writing.

In summary, correlative conjunctions are pairs of words or phrases that connect equal elements in a sentence, creating balanced and parallel structures. They are valuable tools for expressing choices, contrasts, and relationships between ideas, while also emphasizing specific information within a sentence. Understanding and correctly using correlative conjunctions can enhance the clarity and coherence of your writing.

10-4

Connectors in Writing and Speaking

Connectors, also known as transitional words or phrases, play a crucial role in both writing and speaking. They are linguistic devices that help establish relationships between different ideas, sentences, or paragraphs, making your communication smoother, more coherent, and easier to follow. Connectors are essential for effective communication, as they guide your audience through your thoughts and arguments. Here's a comprehensive explanation of connectors in writing and speaking:

PURPOSE OF CONNECTORS:
1. **Coherence**: Connectors improve the overall coherence of your text or speech by linking ideas together logically. They help your audience follow your message without getting lost or confused.

2. **Clarity**: They clarify the relationships between various elements in your text or speech, making it easier for your audience to understand your message.

3. **Emphasis**: Connectors can emphasize certain points or ideas, highlighting their importance in your communication.

4. **Smooth Flow**: They contribute to a smooth and natural flow of information, preventing your writing or speech from feeling disjointed or choppy.

TYPES OF CONNECTORS:

Connectors can be broadly categorized into several types, each serving a specific function:

1. **Addition**: These connectors add information or ideas to what has been previously mentioned.
    - Examples: "Furthermore," "Moreover," "In addition," "Also," "Besides."

2. **Contrast**: These connectors show a difference or contrast between two ideas or pieces of information.
    - Examples: "However," "On the other hand," "Nevertheless," "In contrast," "Although."

3. **Cause and Effect**: These connectors indicate a cause-and-effect relationship between ideas or events.

- Examples: "Because," "Therefore," "Consequently," "As a result," "Hence."

4. **Comparison**: These connectors highlight similarities or draw comparisons between ideas.
   - Examples: "Similarly," "Likewise," "In the same way," "Compared to," "Just as."

5. **Time**: These connectors provide information about the sequence of events or the timing of actions.
   - Examples: "Firstly," "Subsequently," "Meanwhile," "Eventually," "Simultaneously."

6. **Illustration**: These connectors help you provide examples or clarify your point.
   - Examples: "For example," "For instance," "In particular," "To illustrate," "Such as."

7. **Summary or Conclusion**: These connectors signal that you are summarizing or concluding your argument or narrative.
   - Examples: "In conclusion," "To sum up," "In summary," "Therefore," "Overall."

USAGE TIPS FOR CONNECTORS:
1. **Placement**: Connectors can appear at the beginning, middle, or end of a sentence, depending on their role and the overall flow of your writing or speech.

2. **Punctuation**: In formal writing, connectors are often followed by a comma, semicolon, or colon, depending on the specific connector and the sentence's structure.

3. **Variety**: Avoid using the same connectors repeatedly. A diverse range of connectors makes your writing or speech more engaging and less repetitive.

4. **Context**: Choose connectors that best fit the context and the relationships between the ideas you are trying to convey.

EXAMPLES:
- **Writing**: "Furthermore, research indicates that regular exercise can reduce the risk of chronic diseases. Moreover, it has been shown to improve mental health."

- **Speaking**: "On the one hand, we have seen a rise in urbanization. On the other hand, rural areas continue to face population decline."

Connectors are indispensable tools in both writing and speaking. They enhance the clarity, coherence, and overall effectiveness of your communication by linking ideas, showing relationships, and guiding your audience through your message. To improve your communication skills, it's essential to understand the various types of connectors and how to use them appropriately in different contexts.

Chapter 11

Complex Sentences and Clauses

11-1

Dependent vs. Independent Clauses

Dependent and independent clauses are fundamental components of sentence structure in the English language. They are used to construct sentences with various levels of complexity and convey meaning effectively. Here's an explanation of each:

1. Independent Clause:
    - An independent clause, also known as a main clause, is a group of words that forms a complete thought and can stand alone as a sentence.
    - It contains a subject (who or what the sentence is about) and a predicate (what the subject does or what happens to it).
    - Independent clauses express complete ideas and make sense on their own.
    - Example: "She is studying for her final exams."

* * *

2. Dependent Clause:
    - A dependent clause, also called a subordinate clause, is a group of words that does not express a complete thought and cannot stand alone as a sentence.
    - It also contains a subject and a predicate, but it depends on an independent clause to provide context and meaning.
    - Dependent clauses often start with subordinating conjunctions like "because," "although," "while," "since," "if," etc.
    - Example: "Because she is studying for her final exams..."

In the example above, "She is studying for her final exams" is an independent clause, while "Because she is studying for her final exams" is a dependent clause. The dependent clause does not provide a complete idea and relies on the independent clause to give it meaning. Together, they can form a complex sentence like this:

"Because she is studying for her final exams, she has little time for other activities."

In this complex sentence, the dependent clause "Because she is studying for her final exams" provides additional information that helps explain why she has little time for other activities, and the independent clause "she has little time for other activities" forms a complete thought on its own.

Understanding the distinction between dependent and independent clauses is essential for constructing clear and grammatically correct sentences, as it allows you to create various sentence structures and convey different levels of information.

11-2

Types of Subordinate Clauses

Subordinate clauses, also known as dependent clauses, are groups of words that have both a subject and a verb but cannot stand alone as complete sentences. They function within a sentence to provide additional information or to connect ideas. There are several types of subordinate clauses based on their functions and the relationships they establish within a sentence. Here are some common types:

1. **Adjective Clauses (Relative Clauses)**: These clauses provide more information about a noun in the main clause. They are usually introduced by relative pronouns like "who," "whom," "whose," "which," or "that." For example:
    - The book that you lent me is fascinating.
    - The person who won the race is my friend.

2. **Adverb Clauses:** These clauses modify a verb, adjective, or adverb in the main clause and often answer questions like "when," "where," "why," "how," or "to what extent." They are introduced by subordinating conjunctions like "because," "although," "while," "when," "where," and "since." For example:
   - She studied hard because she wanted to get good grades.
   - He went to the store after he finished his homework.

3. **Noun Clauses:** These clauses function as nouns within a sentence, often as subjects, objects, or complements. They are introduced by words like "that," "whether," "if," "what," and "who." For example:
   - What you said is true. (Noun clause as the subject)
   - I don't know if she will come. (Noun clause as the direct object)

4. **Conditional Clauses:** These clauses express a condition that must be met for something else to happen. They typically begin with words like "if," "unless," "provided that," or "whether." For example:
   - If it rains, we will stay inside.
   - She will come unless she is busy.

5. **Purpose Clauses:** These clauses indicate the purpose or intention behind an action. They are often introduced

by words like "so that," "in order that," or "to." For example:
- He worked hard so that he could pass the exam.
- She went to the store to buy some groceries.

6. **Result Clauses:** These clauses show the result or consequence of an action. They are introduced by words like "so...that," "such...that," or "so much/many...that." For example:
   - It was such a hot day that we decided to go swimming.
   - He was so tired that he fell asleep immediately.

7. **Time Clauses:** These clauses indicate when an action in the main clause occurs. They are introduced by subordinating conjunctions like "when," "while," "as," "before," "after," and "since." For example:
   - I will call you when I get home.
   - She left before the movie started.

These are some of the common types of subordinate clauses, but there are others as well. Subordinate clauses add depth and complexity to sentences by providing additional information and creating relationships between ideas within a sentence.

11-3

Complex Sentences in TESOL

Complex sentences play a crucial role in teaching English to speakers of other languages (TESOL) as they help learners understand and communicate ideas at a higher level of sophistication and coherence. Complex sentences are formed by combining independent clauses (complete sentences) and dependent clauses (incomplete sentences) using various subordinating conjunctions and relative pronouns. Here are some key points about complex sentences in TESOL:

1. **Teaching Structure**: When introducing complex sentences, it's essential to start with the basics. Teach students about the structure of complex sentences, including the main clause (independent clause) and the subordinate clause (dependent clause). Make sure they understand how these parts work together.

2. **Subordinating Conjunctions**: Teach students a variety of subordinating conjunctions such as "although," "because," "while," "unless," and "if." These words are used to introduce dependent clauses, indicating the relationship between the clauses.

3. **Relative Pronouns**: Similarly, introduce relative pronouns like "who," "which," and "that," which are used to create adjective clauses within complex sentences. These clauses provide additional information about a noun.

4. **Purpose of Complex Sentences**: Explain to students why complex sentences are essential in English. They allow for greater precision and detail in expressing ideas, making communication more sophisticated and nuanced.

5. **Sentence Combining**: Encourage students to practice creating complex sentences by combining simple sentences. This can be done through various activities and exercises. For example, give them two simple sentences and ask them to create a complex sentence using a subordinating conjunction.

6. **Reading and Analysis**: Provide students with texts that contain complex sentences. Ask them to read and analyze these sentences to understand how they work in context. This helps students see real-world examples of complex sentences in use.

7. **Writing Practice**: Assign writing tasks that require students to use complex sentences. This could involve writing essays, reports, or stories that require them to incorporate complex sentence structures.

8. **Error Correction**: When reviewing students' written work, pay attention to their use of complex sentences. Provide feedback and corrections to help them improve their sentence structures.

9. **Oral Practice**: Encourage students to use complex sentences in spoken language as well. Engage them in discussions and debates that require them to express complex ideas using complex sentence structures.

10. **Progressive Complexity**: As students become more proficient, introduce more complex sentence structures, such as compound-complex sentences, which involve multiple independent and dependent clauses.

11. **Contextual Understanding**: Teach students that the choice of complex sentence structure should be driven by the context and the intended meaning. Help them recognize when a complex sentence is more appropriate than a simple one.

Remember that the complexity of sentence structures should be introduced gradually and tailored to the proficiency level of the students. Building a strong foundation in understanding and using complex sentences is an important aspect of language acquisition in TESOL, as it enhances both written and spoken communication skills.

11-4

Teaching Complex Sentences Effectively

Teaching complex sentences effectively can be a crucial aspect of helping students improve their writing and communication skills. Complex sentences are sentences that contain both independent and dependent clauses, providing depth and variety to written and spoken language. Here are some strategies to teach complex sentences effectively:

1. **Start with the Basics:** Begin by explaining the basic components of a complex sentence:
    - **Independent Clause:** A complete sentence that can stand alone.
    - **Dependent Clause:** A group of words with a subject and a verb but cannot stand alone as a sentence.

2. **Show Examples:** Provide clear examples of complex sentences to help students understand the concept.

Break down the sentences into their constituent parts and identify the independent and dependent clauses.

3. **Use Visual Aids:** Visual aids like diagrams or sentence trees can help students visualize the structure of complex sentences. This can make it easier for them to grasp the concept.

4. **Connect to Prior Knowledge:** Relate complex sentences to what students already know about simple sentences and compound sentences. Highlight how complex sentences add depth and detail to writing.

5. **Identify Coordinating Conjunctions:** Teach students about coordinating conjunctions (e.g., and, but, or, so) and how they can be used to combine independent and dependent clauses to create complex sentences.

6. **Introduce Subordinating Conjunctions:** Discuss subordinating conjunctions (e.g., because, although, while, if) and how they are used to introduce dependent clauses in complex sentences.

7. **Practice Sentence Combining:** Provide exercises where students can practice combining simple sentences into complex ones. This can be done through guided activities or independent writing tasks.

8. **Analyze Texts:** Have students analyze complex sentences in literature or non-fiction texts. Ask them to identify the purpose and effect of using complex sentences in those contexts.

9. **Peer Review:** Encourage peer review and editing. Have students review each other's writing to identify and correct issues related to complex sentences.

10. **Provide Feedback:** Offer constructive feedback on students' writing, focusing on their use of complex sentences. Point out where they could improve or where they have used them effectively.

11. **Modeling:** Model the use of complex sentences in your own writing or through examples. Show how they can enhance clarity and expressiveness in communication.

12. **Differentiate Instruction:** Recognize that students may have different levels of proficiency with complex sentences. Differentiate your instruction to meet individual needs.

13. **Continuous Practice:** Complex sentence construction may take time to master. Encourage students to practice regularly in both their writing and speaking.

14. **Contextualize Learning:** Help students understand that the use of complex sentences is context-dependent. Different writing situations may require different sentence structures.

15. **Assessment:** Assess students' understanding and use of complex sentences through quizzes, assignments, and writing assessments. Provide feedback for improvement.

Teaching complex sentences effectively requires patience and consistent practice. Remember to create a supportive learning environment where students feel comfortable experimenting with their writing and asking questions.

Chapter 12

Modal Verbs and Conditional Sentences

12-1

Understanding Modal Verbs

Modal verbs are a special category of verbs in English that are used to indicate the speaker's attitude, likelihood, necessity, permission, ability, or obligation regarding the action or state expressed by the main verb in a sentence. Modal verbs are essential for conveying shades of meaning and expressing various degrees of certainty, possibility, and obligation. In English, there are ten primary modal verbs:

1. Can:
    - Usage: Indicates ability, possibility, or permission.
    - Examples:
        - I can swim. (ability)
        - She can come to the party. (permission)
        - It can rain later. (possibility)

2. Could:
    - Usage: Often used for past ability or polite requests.
    - Examples:

- I could swim when I was five. (past ability)
- Could you please pass the salt? (polite request)

3. **May:**
    - Usage: Indicates permission or possibility.
    - Examples:
        - You may leave the classroom. (permission)
        - It may rain later. (possibility)

4. **Might:**
    - Usage: Similar to 'may,' but implies a lower degree of probability.
    - Examples:
        - He might come to the party. (possibility with lower probability)

5. **Must:**
    - Usage: Indicates necessity or strong obligation.
    - Examples:
        - You must complete the assignment. (necessity)
        - I must go to the doctor. (strong obligation)

6. **Shall:**
    - Usage: Used to make suggestions, offers, or express future actions in formal or British English.
    - Examples:
        - Shall we go to the movies? (suggestion)
        - I shall be there at 3 PM. (future action in British English)

7. Should:
    - Usage: Indicates advice, recommendation, or expectation.
    - Examples:
        - You should eat your vegetables. (recommendation)
        - He should be here by now. (expectation)

8. Will:
    - Usage: Expresses future actions or predictions.
    - Examples:
        - I will call you later. (future action)
        - It will rain tomorrow. (prediction)

9. Would:
    - Usage: Often used for polite requests, hypothetical situations, or expressing preferences.
    - Examples:
        - Would you please pass me the book? (polite request)
        - If I won the lottery, I would travel the world. (hypothetical situation)
        - I would rather stay home tonight. (preference)

10. Ought to:
    - Usage: Indicates moral obligation or strong recommendation.
    - Examples:

- You ought to help your neighbor. (moral obligation)
- You ought to see that movie; it's great. (strong recommendation)

Key points to remember about modal verbs:

1. **Modal verbs do not change with the subject:** They remain the same regardless of whether the subject is singular or plural. For example, "He can swim" and "They can swim" both use "can."

2. **Modal verbs are always followed by the base form of the main verb:** For example, "She can swim," not "She can swims."

3. **Modal verbs do not have tenses:** They do not change to reflect past, present, or future actions. Instead, the meaning is usually inferred from the context.

4. **Modal verbs can be used to form questions, negatives, and statements:** For example, "Can you swim?" (question), "I cannot swim" (negative), and "She can swim" (statement).

5. **Modal verbs are often used to express degrees of certainty and necessity:** For example, "must" indicates a strong necessity, while "might" suggests a lower level of probability.

6. Modal verbs can be used in combination: You can use multiple modal verbs in a sentence to express complex meanings, such as "She must have been studying all night," which combines "must" and "have been."

In summary, understanding modal verbs is essential for effective communication in English. These versatile verbs enable speakers and writers to convey various shades of meaning related to possibility, necessity, ability, and more, adding depth and nuance to the language.

12-2

Using Modal Verbs in TESOL

Modal verbs play an important role in teaching English to speakers of other languages (TESOL) because they express various shades of meaning, necessity, possibility, and ability. They are used to convey nuances in communication and are fundamental for learners to understand and use in both spoken and written English. Here's how modal verbs can be effectively used in TESOL:

1. **Introducing Modal Verbs**: Start by introducing the concept of modal verbs to your students. Explain that these are a special group of auxiliary verbs that modify the meaning of the main verb. Common modal verbs in English include can, could, may, might, must, shall, should, will, and would.

2. **Teaching Functions**: Modal verbs serve various functions in English. Teach your students the different functions, such as expressing possibility,

necessity, ability, permission, and requests. Provide examples and context for each function.

3. **Modal Verb Charts**: Create charts or handouts that show the different modal verbs, their forms, and the functions they can perform. This visual aid can help students understand and remember the information better.

4. **Practice in Context**: Provide contextual examples and exercises for each function of modal verbs. For example:
    - Expressing Possibility: "It might rain tomorrow."
    - Expressing Necessity: "You must study for the exam."
    - Expressing Ability: "She can speak Spanish fluently."
    - Expressing Permission: "You may go to the restroom."
    - Making Requests: "Could you pass me the salt, please?"

5. **Modal Verb Games and Activities**: Incorporate games and activities into your TESOL lessons to make learning modal verbs fun and engaging. For example:
    - Role-Playing: Have students role-play scenarios where they use modal verbs appropriately, such as making requests or giving advice.

- Modal Verb Bingo: Create bingo cards with sentences using modal verbs, and students mark the sentences with the correct modal verb as you call them out.
- Modal Verb Scavenger Hunt: Provide a list of sentences, and students need to find and highlight modal verbs in a text or in a series of sentences.

6. **Modal Verb Challenges**: Challenge advanced learners by introducing more complex uses of modal verbs, such as perfect modals (e.g., could have, must have) and continuous modals (e.g., can be, might be).

7. **Error Correction**: Encourage students to use modal verbs in their written and spoken assignments. Provide feedback on their usage and help them correct any errors.

8. **Real-Life Context**: Show students how modal verbs are used in real-life situations, such as in news articles, advertisements, and conversations. Analyze these examples together to deepen their understanding.

9. **Homework and Practice**: Assign homework exercises or practice activities that focus on modal verbs. This allows students to reinforce what they've learned outside of the classroom.

10. **Assessment**: Include modal verbs in your assessments to gauge students' comprehension and usage. This could include quizzes, tests, or speaking assessments.

Remember that mastering modal verbs can be challenging for English learners, so be patient and provide ample opportunities for practice and reinforcement. Tailor your lessons to the proficiency level of your students, gradually introducing more complex uses of modal verbs as they progress in their language learning journey.

12-3

Conditional Sentences: Zero, First, Second, and Third Conditionals

Conditional sentences, often referred to as "if" sentences, are grammatical structures that express a hypothetical situation and its possible consequences. These sentences are divided into four main types: Zero Conditional, First Conditional, Second Conditional, and Third Conditional.

Each type has its own specific structure and is used to convey different degrees of likelihood or probability. Let's explore each type in detail:

1. Zero Conditional:
    - Structure: If + present simple tense, present simple tense.
    - Usage: The Zero Conditional is used to express general truths, scientific facts, or situations that

are always true. It represents a cause-and-effect relationship where the result is certain and always follows the condition.
  - Example:
    - If you heat water to 100 degrees Celsius, it boils.
    - If it rains, the ground gets wet.

2. First Conditional:
    - Structure: If + present simple tense, will + base form of the verb.
    - Usage: The First Conditional is used to talk about possible future situations that are likely to happen. It implies a realistic or probable outcome based on the condition.
    - Example:
        - If it rains tomorrow, I will stay at home.
        - If she studies hard, she will pass the exam.

3. Second Conditional:
    - Structure: If + past simple tense, would + base form of the verb.
    - Usage: The Second Conditional is used to talk about hypothetical or unreal situations in the present or future. It implies that the condition is unlikely or not true in reality.
    - Example:
        - If I won the lottery, I would buy a new car.
        - If he were here, he would help us.

4. Third Conditional:
    - Structure: If + past perfect tense, would have + past participle.
    - Usage: The Third Conditional is used to talk about unreal situations in the past. It describes events that did not happen and their hypothetical outcomes.
    - Example:
        - If I had known you were coming, I would have baked a cake.
        - If they had studied harder, they would have passed the test.

Additional Notes:

- In the First Conditional, you can use "will" or other modal verbs like "can," "may," or "might" to express the consequence.
- In the Second Conditional, you can also use "could," "might," or "should" instead of "would" in some cases.
- In the Third Conditional, "could have," "might have," or "should have" can replace "would have" depending on the context.

It's important to note that these conditional sentences can be mixed and modified to express more nuanced meanings. Additionally, the use of the past tense forms in the Second and Third Conditionals can vary based on context, such as using "were" instead of "was" for all subjects in the Second Conditional to indicate extreme improbability (subjunctive mood). Mastery of conditional sentences allows for effective communication of various hypothetical scenarios and their potential outcomes.

12-4

Teaching Modals and Conditionals

Teaching modals and conditionals is an essential part of English language instruction. Modals are auxiliary verbs that express various degrees of necessity, possibility, permission, ability, and obligation, while conditionals are used to talk about hypothetical situations and their potential consequences. Here's a step-by-step guide on how to teach modals and conditionals effectively:

1. Understand the Basics:
    - Make sure you have a solid understanding of modals and conditionals yourself before teaching them. This includes knowing the different modal verbs and how they are used, as well as the various types of conditional sentences.

2. Plan Your Lessons:
    - Break down your lessons into manageable chunks. Focus on one type of modal or

conditional at a time to avoid overwhelming your students.

3. **Introduce Modals:**
   - Start with the basics by introducing the common modal verbs such as can, could, may, might, must, shall, should, will, would.
   - Explain their meanings and uses. For example, can for ability, may for permission, must for obligation, etc.

4. **Practice Modals:**
   - Provide examples and practice exercises for each modal verb separately. This could include fill-in-the-blank exercises, role-playing scenarios, or discussions.

5. **Introduce Conditionals:**
   - Begin with the zero, first, and second conditionals, as they are the most commonly used.
   - Explain the structure of conditional sentences, including the if-clause (condition) and the main clause (result).

6. **Practice Conditionals:**
   - Provide examples and practice exercises for each type of conditional sentence. Use real- life situations to make it more engaging.
   - Encourage students to create their own conditional sentences.

7. Use Real-Life Examples:
    - Incorporate real-life examples, news articles, or stories that use modals and conditionals to illustrate their practical use in everyday communication.

8. Discuss Nuances:
    - Talk about the nuances and differences between modal verbs. For example, the difference between "can" and "could," or "must" and "have to."

9. Role-Playing and Scenarios:
    - Engage students in role-playing scenarios that require the use of modals and conditionals. This can help them practice in a more interactive way.

10. Correct and Give Feedback:
    - Correct students' mistakes gently and provide constructive feedback. Encourage peer review and self-assessment as well.

11. Gradually Introduce Advanced Concepts:
    - As students become comfortable with the basics, introduce more complex topics such as third conditionals, mixed conditionals, and modal verbs in the passive voice.

12. Encourage Speaking and Writing:
    - Encourage students to incorporate modals and conditionals into their spoken and written communication. Provide opportunities for them to use these structures in discussions, essays, and presentations.

13. Review and Practice Regularly:
    - Schedule regular review sessions to reinforce the concepts learned and to address any lingering questions or issues.

14. Provide Additional Resources:
    - Recommend textbooks, online resources, and grammar exercises for students to practice independently.

Remember that teaching modals and conditionals can be challenging for some learners, so patience and repetition are key. Tailor your lessons to the specific needs and proficiency levels of your students, and adjust your teaching methods accordingly.

Chapter 13

Passive Voice and Reported Speech

13-1

Passive Voice: Formation and USE

Passive voice is a grammatical construction that emphasizes the action done to the subject of a sentence rather than the subject performing the action. It is formed by changing the word order and the verb form. In English, passive voice is often used when the doer of the action is either unknown or less important than the action itself.

Here is how passive voice is formed and used:

Formation:

1. Passive Voice with the Simple Present Tense:
    - **Active:** The chef prepares the meal.
    - **Passive:** The meal is prepared by the chef.
    In the passive voice, the subject of the active voice sentence (the chef) becomes the agent introduced by "by" (or sometimes "with" or other prepositions), and the object of the active voice sentence (the meal) becomes the subject of the passive voice sentence.

2. Passive Voice with the Simple Past Tense:
    - Active: The team won the game.
    - Passive: The game was won by the team.

3. Passive Voice with the Future Tense:
    - Active: They will finish the project tomorrow.
    - Passive: The project will be finished tomorrow.

4. Passive Voice with Modal Verbs (e.g., can, must, should):
    - Active: You must complete the assignment.
    - Passive: The assignment must be completed.

Use:

1. When the doer is unknown or unimportant: Passive voice can be used when you don't know or don't want to emphasize who performed the action.
    - Passive: The book was stolen.

2. To emphasize the action or the result: Passive voice can shift the focus to what happened rather than who did it.
    - Passive: The Mona Lisa was painted in the 16th century.

3. In formal or scientific writing: Passive voice is often used in academic, scientific, or technical writing to maintain objectivity and focus on the facts.

- **Passive:** The experiment was conducted under controlled conditions.

4. **When the receiver of the action is more important:** Sometimes, passive voice is used to put more emphasis on the entity that received the action rather than the one who performed it.
    - **Passive:** The new hospital was built to serve the community.

5. **To avoid blame or responsibility:** Passive voice can be used to avoid assigning blame or responsibility directly.
    - **Passive:** Mistakes were made.

It's important to note that while passive voice has its uses, it should not be overused. In many cases, active voice is more direct and concise, so choose the voice that best suits your communication goals and context.

13-2

Teaching Passive Voice

Teaching passive voice can be a challenging yet important aspect of English language instruction. Passive voice is a grammatical structure where the subject of a sentence receives the action, rather than performing the action. Here's a step-by-step guide on how to teach passive voice effectively:

1. **Introduce the Concept:** Start by explaining what passive voice is and why it's used in English. Emphasize that it's used to shift the focus from the doer of the action (the subject) to the receiver of the action (the object).

2. **Provide Examples:** Show clear examples of active and passive voice sentences. Compare them to illustrate the difference. For instance:
    - Active: "The cat chased the mouse."
    - Passive: "The mouse was chased by the cat."

3. **Identify the Components:** Break down passive voice sentences into their components: subject, verb, and object. Highlight that the object in the active voice sentence becomes the subject in the passive voice sentence.

4. **Explain the Formula:** Present the passive voice formula: "Subject + to be (conjugated) + past participle (usually the main verb in the past participle form) + by + agent (optional)." Explain that the agent (the doer of the action) is only included if it's important to know or specify who performed the action.

5. **Practice Conjugation:** Review the various forms of the verb "to be" (am, is, are, was, were) and how they are used with different subjects (I am, he/she/it is, we/you/they are). Practice conjugating "to be" with different subjects.

6. **Practice with Regular and Irregular Verbs:** Discuss the use of past participles, both regular (e.g., worked, played) and irregular (e.g., eaten, written). Provide examples and practice exercises with a variety of verbs.

7. **Active to Passive Transformation:** Teach how to transform active voice sentences into passive voice sentences:

- Identify the object of the active sentence.
- Make it the subject of the passive sentence.
- Use the appropriate form of "to be."
- Use the past participle of the main verb.
- Add "by + agent" if necessary.

8. **Practice Exercises:** Provide plenty of exercises and worksheets for students to practice transforming sentences from active to passive voice and vice versa. Encourage them to identify the passive voice in reading materials.

9. **Discuss When to Use Passive Voice:** Explain when passive voice is commonly used, such as in formal writing, when the doer of the action is unknown or unimportant, or to create variety in writing.

10. **Examples from Real Texts:** Show examples of passive voice in real-world contexts, such as news articles, academic papers, and literature. Discuss why authors might choose to use passive voice in those situations.

11. **Errors and Common Mistakes:** Address common mistakes students make when using passive voice, such as incorrect conjugation of "to be" or confusion with active voice.

12. **Homework and Review:** Assign homework exercises and periodically review passive voice in subsequent lessons to reinforce learning.

13. **Assessment:** Assess students' understanding of passive voice through quizzes, tests, or writing assignments.

Remember that learning passive voice takes time and practice, so be patient with your students and provide ample opportunities for them to apply what they've learned in their own writing and speaking.

13-3

Reported Speech: Direct and INdirect Speech

Reported speech, also known as indirect speech, is a fundamental aspect of grammar used to convey someone else's words, thoughts, or ideas without quoting them directly. It allows speakers and writers to report what someone else has said while integrating it into their own sentences. There are two primary ways to convey reported speech: direct speech and indirect speech.

1. **Direct Speech**: Direct speech involves quoting the exact words spoken by a person within quotation marks. For example:
    - She said, "I am going to the store."
    In this example, the speaker directly quotes what "she" said, enclosing the statement in quotation marks to distinguish it from their own words.
    Key features of direct speech:

- Uses quotation marks (" ") to enclose the spoken words.
- Preserves the original speaker's exact words, including tense, pronouns, and verb forms.
- Often used in dialogue, interviews, and storytelling to add realism and directness.

2. **Indirect Speech (Reported Speech)**: Indirect speech, also known as reported speech, involves paraphrasing or reporting what someone else said without quoting their exact words. It often requires changes in pronouns, verb tenses, and word order to make the reported speech fit seamlessly into the reporting sentence. For example:
    - She said that she was going to the store.
      In this example, the speaker reports what "she" said without quoting the exact words. This requires changes in the verb tense ("am" changes to "was") and the introduction of a reporting clause ("She said that...").
      Key features of indirect speech:
    - Typically does not use quotation marks.
    - Requires changes in verb tenses and pronouns to fit the context of the reporting sentence.
    - Often introduced by reporting verbs like "said," "told," "asked," or "explained."
    - Commonly used in news reporting, storytelling, and academic writing.

Important Rules and Transformations for Indirect Speech:

1. **Change of Pronouns:**
    - In indirect speech, pronouns often change to reflect the perspective of the reporting speaker. For example, "I" may become "she," and "you" may become "he."

2. **Change of Verb Tenses:**
    - Present simple changes to past simple.
    - Present continuous changes to past continuous.
    - Present perfect changes to past perfect.
    - Will changes to would.
    - Can changes to could.
    - Must changes to had to, etc.

3. **Backshift of Time Expressions:**
    - Time expressions often shift to reflect that the reported speech is no longer in the present but is now being reported in the past. For example, "today" becomes "that day," and "now" becomes "then."

4. **Reporting Verbs:**
    - Reporting verbs like "said," "told," "asked," etc., are used to introduce reported speech and can influence the structure of the sentence.

5. **Omission of Quotation Marks:**

- Unlike direct speech, indirect speech does not use quotation marks to enclose the reported words.

6. Reporting Clauses:
    - Indirect speech is often introduced by a reporting clause (e.g., "He said that..."), which connects the reported speech to the rest of the sentence.

In summary, reported speech, or indirect speech, is a way of conveying what someone else has said while integrating it into one's own sentences. It involves changes in pronouns, verb tenses, and word order to make the reported speech grammatically and contextually appropriate within the reporting sentence. Understanding the rules and transformations associated with reported speech is crucial for effective communication in both spoken and written English.

13-4

Teaching Reported Speech

Teaching reported speech, also known as indirect speech, is an important aspect of teaching English grammar. Reported speech is used to report what someone else has said without quoting their exact words. Here's a step-by-step guide on how to teach reported speech effectively:

1. **Introduce the Concept**: Start by explaining what reported speech is and why it is used. Emphasize that it is used to convey what someone else has said in a more indirect manner.

2. **Direct vs. Reported Speech**: Differentiate between direct speech (quoting the speaker's exact words) and reported speech. Provide examples to illustrate the difference.
    - Direct Speech: She said, "I am going to the store."
    - Reported Speech: She said that she was going to the store.

3. **Tense Changes**: Discuss how verb tenses change when converting from direct to reported speech. Common changes include:
    - Present simple ➡ Past simple
    - Present continuous ➡ Past continuous
    - Present perfect ➡ Past perfect

    Provide examples and practice exercises to reinforce these changes.

4. **Pronoun Changes**: Explain how pronouns change in reported speech to reflect the perspective of the reporting speaker. For instance:
    - She said, "I am busy." ➡ She said that she was busy.

    Reinforce the idea that "I" becomes "she," and the pronoun shift is necessary.

5. **Reporting Verbs**: Teach students about common reporting verbs like "say," "tell," "ask," and "explain." Discuss how these verbs are used to introduce reported speech.
    - She said, "I'll be late." ➡ She told me that she would be late.

6. **Time and Place Expressions**: Explain how time and place expressions (now, here, today, tomorrow, etc.) may change or remain the same when reporting speech. Provide examples.
    - "I'm coming tomorrow," she said. ➡ She said she was coming tomorrow.

7. **Backshifting**: Discuss the concept of backshifting, where verbs often shift one tense back in reported speech. Practice this with various tenses.

8. **Practice Exercises**: Provide plenty of exercises for students to practice converting direct speech into reported speech. Include a variety of tenses, pronouns, and reporting verbs.

9. **Role-Play and Conversations**: Engage students in role-play activities and conversations where they have to report what others have said. This makes the learning experience more interactive and practical.

10. **Assessment**: Assess students' understanding through quizzes, written assignments, or speaking activities. Provide feedback and correct any mistakes.

11. **Common Mistakes**: Address common errors that students make when using reported speech and emphasize the importance of accuracy.

12. **Real-Life Examples**: Show how reported speech is used in real-life situations like news reports, interviews, and storytelling.

13. **Advanced Concepts** (optional): For more advanced learners, introduce concepts like reporting questions, requests, and imperatives.

Remember that teaching reported speech is a gradual process, and students may need time to grasp the concept fully. Be patient, provide ample practice, and encourage students to use reported speech in their own writing and conversations to reinforce their learning.

Chapter 14

Common Grammar Pitfalls

14-1

Most Common ESL Grammar Errors

English as a Second Language (ESL) learners often make specific grammar errors that are common across various language backgrounds. Here are some of the most common ESL grammar errors:

1. **Subject-Verb Agreement**: This occurs when the subject and verb in a sentence do not agree in terms of number (singular or plural). For example:
    - Incorrect: "The book are on the table."
    - Correct: "The book is on the table."

2. **Verb Tense**: ESL learners sometimes struggle with using the correct verb tense in sentences. For example:
    - Incorrect: "I will go to the store yesterday."
    - Correct: "I went to the store yesterday."

3. **Articles (a, an, the)**: Misusing articles or omitting them is a common error.
    - Incorrect: "I saw a movie yesterday."
    - Correct: "I saw the movie yesterday."

4. **Pluralization**: Making nouns plural incorrectly can be problematic.
    - Incorrect: "She has two childs."
    - Correct: "She has two children."

5. **Word Order**: The word order in English can be different from other languages. For instance, in English, the order is typically subject-verb-object.
    - Incorrect: "I gave him the book yesterday."
    - Correct: "I gave the book to him yesterday."

6. **Prepositions**: Incorrect use of prepositions can lead to errors.
    - Incorrect: "I'm good in cooking."
    - Correct: "I'm good at cooking."

7. **Pronoun Usage**: Misusing or omitting pronouns is a common mistake.
    - Incorrect: "She is my sister. She is very kind."
    - Correct: "She is my sister, and she is very kind."

8. **Negation**: Misplacing or omitting negations can change the meaning of a sentence.
    - Incorrect: "I don't want to go nowhere."

- Correct: "I don't want to go anywhere."

9. **Word Choice**: Choosing the wrong word or phrase can result in grammatical errors.
    - Incorrect: "I am interesting in learning English."
    - Correct: "I am interested in learning English."

10. **Run-on Sentences**: ESL learners may struggle with joining sentences correctly.
    - Incorrect: "I like coffee it helps me stay awake."
    - Correct: "I like coffee because it helps me stay awake."

11. **Double Negatives**: In English, double negatives cancel each other out.
    - Incorrect: "I don't need no help."
    - Correct: "I don't need any help."

12. **Agreement in Comparative and Superlative Forms**: Making mistakes in comparative and superlative forms of adjectives.
    - Incorrect: "He is the most tallest person in the room."
    - Correct: "He is the tallest person in the room."

13. **Incomplete Sentences**: Leaving out essential parts of a sentence.
    - Incorrect: "Eating lunch."
    - Correct: "I am eating lunch."

14. **Parallel Structure**: Failing to maintain parallelism when listing items in a series.
    - Incorrect: "She likes to dance, sing, and reading."
    - Correct: "She likes to dance, sing, and read."

15. **Modal Verbs**: Misusing modal verbs like can, could, should, must.
    - Incorrect: "I can to swim."
    - Correct: "I can swim."

16. **Relative Clauses**: Difficulty in forming relative clauses.
    - Incorrect: "The girl who I met her is my friend."
    - Correct: "The girl whom I met is my friend."

These errors are typical among ESL learners but can vary depending on their native language and proficiency level. It's important to note that making mistakes is a natural part of learning, and with practice and guidance, ESL learners can improve their grammar skills.

14-2

Strategies for Error Correction

Error correction is an essential aspect of teaching English grammar, as it helps learners identify and rectify mistakes in their language usage. Here are some strategies for effective error correction in teaching English grammar:

1. Immediate Feedback:
    - Correct errors as soon as they occur during a speaking or writing activity. This helps learners associate the correction with the specific context in which the mistake was made.

2. Balance Positive and Negative Feedback:
    - Provide positive reinforcement for correct usage, as it boosts learners' confidence.
    - When correcting errors, be constructive and sensitive to avoid demotivating students.

3. Error Types:

- Categorize errors into different types, such as grammatical, vocabulary, or pronunciation errors. Address each type appropriately.

4. **Error Identification:**
    - Encourage self-correction by asking students to identify and correct their own mistakes before you intervene.

5. **Error Logs:**
    - Have students keep error logs, where they record mistakes they make during class or homework. Review these logs periodically to track progress and address recurring issues.

6. **Peer Correction:**
    - Encourage peer correction during group activities or peer review sessions. This promotes collaborative learning and allows students to learn from each other.

7. **Delayed Correction:**
    - Sometimes, it's beneficial to delay error correction until after an activity to avoid interrupting the flow of communication. Review and discuss errors as a group afterwards.

8. **Codes and Symbols:**

- Use codes or symbols (e.g., underline for grammar, circle for vocabulary) to mark errors in written work. Ask students to decipher and correct them themselves.

9. Focus on Priority Errors:
    - Identify and prioritize common errors that significantly impact communication. Concentrate on correcting these errors first.

10. Error Analysis:
    - Conduct error analysis sessions where you discuss specific patterns of mistakes that students commonly make and work on them collectively.

11. Model Correct Usage:
    - Provide examples of correct usage, both written and spoken, to help students understand the right way to express themselves.

12. Error Correction Games:
    - Integrate error correction into fun activities and games, making it an engaging and interactive learning experience.

13. Error Correction Worksheets:
    - Create worksheets or exercises specifically designed for error correction. These can be used for self-study or group activities.

14. **Encourage Questions:**
    - Create a classroom environment where students feel comfortable asking questions about language usage. Address these questions as they arise.

15. **Focus on Communication:**
    - While grammar is important, emphasize the importance of effective communication. Encourage students to prioritize clarity and fluency over perfection.

16. **Use Technology:**
    - Utilize grammar-checking tools and language-learning apps to supplement your teaching. These tools can provide immediate feedback and practice opportunities.

17. **Progressive Correction:**
    - Gradually increase the complexity of correction as students become more proficient. Start with basic errors and move on to more advanced ones.

18. **Individualized Correction:**
    - Recognize that different students may have different error patterns. Tailor your correction strategies to address the specific needs of each learner.

Remember that error correction should be a supportive and constructive process that helps students improve their language skills without discouraging them. The goal is to create a positive and effective learning experience.

14-3

Prompting Self-Correction

Promoting self-correction in teaching English grammar is an essential aspect of helping learners become more proficient in the language. Self-correction not only fosters independent learning but also encourages critical thinking and problem-solving skills. Here are some strategies to promote self-correction in your English grammar teaching:

1. Error Awareness:
    - Encourage students to be aware of their own errors by highlighting the importance of accurate grammar.
    - Use self-assessment tools like checklists or error logs where students can track their mistakes.

2. Peer Review:
    - Incorporate peer review sessions where students review and correct each other's written work or spoken responses.

- Provide guidelines for effective peer feedback, emphasizing constructive criticism.

3. **Immediate Feedback:**
   - Offer immediate feedback during class discussions or exercises to address errors as they occur.
   - Explain why a particular grammar rule applies and how to correct the mistake.

4. **Self-Editing Exercises:**
   - Assign self-editing tasks where students review and correct their own written work before submitting it.
   - Provide clear guidelines and a checklist for common grammar errors.

5. **Error Analysis:**
   - Encourage students to analyze their own errors by identifying patterns and recurring mistakes.
   - Have them keep a record of frequently occurring errors and work on improving them.

6. **Gamification:**
   - Use grammar games and quizzes that require students to identify and correct errors in sentences.
   - Make it competitive and rewarding to motivate students to self-correct.

7. **Model Correcting Techniques:**
    - Demonstrate how to correct grammar errors effectively, showing different methods such as proofreading, using grammar reference books, or seeking help online.

8. **Socratic Questioning:**
    - Engage students in discussions by asking questions that lead them to identify and correct grammar mistakes in their own or others' sentences.
    - Encourage them to explain why certain corrections are needed.

9. **Error Logs:**
    - Ask students to maintain an error log where they record their grammar mistakes along with corrections and explanations.
    - Review these logs periodically to track progress.

10. **Reflective Journals:**
    - Assign reflective writing tasks where students analyze their language use, identify errors, and propose solutions.
    - Encourage them to set goals for improvement based on their reflections.

11. **Encourage Resource Use:**

- Teach students how to use grammar reference materials, online tools, and grammar-check software effectively.
- Promote self-sufficiency in seeking help when needed.

12. **Progressive Assessments:**
    - Implement a progressive assessment system that focuses on continuous improvement. Allow students to correct and resubmit assignments to earn better grades.

13. **Celebrate Improvement:**
    - Recognize and celebrate students' progress in self-correction, reinforcing the idea that making mistakes is a part of learning.

Promoting self-correction in teaching English grammar may require patience and consistent effort, but it can significantly enhance students' language skills and their ability to become more independent learners. Encouraging a growth mindset, where students view errors as opportunities for improvement, is also crucial in this process.

Chapter 15

Teaching Grammar Effectively

15-1

Communicative Language Teaching (CLT)

Communicative Language Teaching (CLT) is an approach to language teaching that emphasizes communication and the use of language in real-life situations. While CLT places a strong emphasis on developing speaking and listening skills, it also incorporates the teaching of grammar in a way that is contextually relevant and functional. Here's how CLT approaches teaching English grammar:

1. Grammar as a Tool:
    - In CLT, grammar is viewed as a tool to facilitate communication rather than an end in itself. Learners are encouraged to use grammar structures to express themselves effectively in various communicative contexts.

2. Contextual Learning:

- Grammar is taught within meaningful and authentic contexts. Instead of isolated grammar exercises, learners encounter grammar structures in texts, dialogues, and situations that mirror real-life language use.

3. Communicative Activities:
    - Grammar is often introduced or practiced through communicative activities such as role-plays, debates, discussions, and problem-solving tasks. These activities require students to use grammar structures to convey messages and achieve specific goals.

4. Error Tolerance:
    - CLT recognizes that learners may make grammatical errors as they communicate. Rather than focusing solely on error correction, CLT encourages teachers to provide feedback that helps students improve their communication skills while being tolerant of minor errors.

5. Inductive Learning:
    - CLT often employs an inductive approach to grammar teaching. Instead of explicitly teaching rules, students are encouraged to discover and internalize grammar patterns through exposure and practice.

6. Focus on Meaning:

- In CLT, the emphasis is on understanding the meaning of grammar structures and how they contribute to effective communication. Learners are encouraged to use grammar rules in context to convey messages accurately.

7. Learner-Centered:
    - CLT is learner-centered, allowing students to have a more active role in their language learning. Students are encouraged to explore and experiment with language, helping them develop a deeper understanding of grammar.

8. Authentic Materials:
    - Teachers often incorporate authentic materials such as newspapers, magazines, videos, and real-world conversations to expose students to natural language use, including authentic grammar patterns.

9. Task-Based Learning:
    - Task-based language learning is a common practice within CLT. Students work on tasks that require the application of grammar knowledge to complete a specific goal, making the learning experience more meaningful.

10. Form-Focused Instruction:
    - While CLT focuses on communication, there is still room for form-focused instruction when needed.

Teachers may address specific grammar points or errors that impede effective communication during or after communicative activities.

In summary, CLT integrates the teaching of English grammar into meaningful communication contexts, with a strong emphasis on the practical use of language. It encourages learners to become proficient communicators by using grammar as a tool to convey meaning effectively in real-life situations.

15-2

Integrating Grammar into Lessons

Integrating grammar into lessons effectively is crucial for improving students' language skills. Here are some strategies and tips to help you integrate grammar instruction seamlessly into your lessons:

1. **Contextualization:** Present grammar concepts in real-life contexts. Show students how the grammar point is used in conversations, texts, or situations they can relate to. This makes grammar more relevant and memorable.

2. **Use Authentic Materials:** Incorporate authentic materials such as news articles, podcasts, or videos that naturally showcase the use of grammar in real-world communication. Discuss and analyze these materials with your students.

3. **Integrated Skills**: Combine grammar instruction with other language skills like reading, writing, speaking, and listening. For example, when teaching verb tenses, have students read a short passage, identify the tenses used, and then discuss the passage or write a summary.

4. **Games and Activities**: Engage students in grammar-focused games and activities. Activities like crossword puzzles, word searches, board games, or online quizzes can make learning grammar fun and interactive.

5. **Interactive Exercises**: Use interactive exercises that allow students to practice grammar in context. Interactive whiteboards, online grammar quizzes, and grammar-checking tools can be helpful.

6. **Error Analysis**: Have students analyze and correct sentences with grammatical errors. This helps them identify common mistakes and reinforces correct usage.

7. **Peer Editing**: Encourage students to peer-edit each other's writing assignments. This not only improves their grammar but also enhances their editing skills.

8. **Grammar in Writing:** When teaching writing, focus on one or two specific grammar points that are relevant to the writing task. Provide feedback on how well students apply those grammar rules in their compositions.

9. **Grammar Journals:** Have students keep a grammar journal where they record new grammar concepts, examples from their reading, and their own writing. This serves as a personal reference tool.

10. **Scaffolded Learning:** Start with simple grammar concepts and gradually introduce more complex ones as students progress. Build on their existing knowledge to avoid overwhelming them.

11. **Differentiated Instruction:** Recognize that students may have different levels of grammar proficiency. Differentiate your instruction by offering extra support to those who need it and more challenging tasks to advanced learners.

12. **Regular Practice:** Consistency is key. Include regular grammar practice in your lesson plans to reinforce concepts over time.

13. **Formative Assessment:** Use formative assessments, such as quizzes or in-class activities, to gauge students'

understanding of grammar concepts. Adjust your instruction based on their performance.

14. **Feedback:** Provide constructive feedback on students' grammar errors. Encourage them to learn from their mistakes and apply corrections in future assignments.

15. **Integration with Literature:** If applicable, connect grammar lessons to the literature you're studying in class. Analyze how authors use grammar to convey meaning and style.

16. **Cultural Context:** When teaching grammar in a foreign language, consider cultural differences in language use. This helps students understand the nuances of grammar in different contexts.

17. **Student-Centered Learning:** Encourage students to take an active role in their learning. Ask them to research and present on specific grammar topics or lead grammar discussions in class.

Remember that integrating grammar into lessons should not be isolated from the broader language learning process. It should complement other language skills and be part of a holistic approach to language education. Furthermore, adapt your strategies to the age, proficiency level, and specific needs of your students to ensure effective grammar instruction.

15-3

Using Authentic Materials

Using authentic materials in teaching English grammar can be a highly effective way to engage students and make the learning process more meaningful and practical. Authentic materials refer to real-world texts and resources that are not specifically created for language learners. They can include newspapers, magazines, advertisements, songs, movie scripts, websites, and more. Here are some tips on how to effectively use authentic materials in teaching English grammar:

1. **Select Relevant Materials**: Choose authentic materials that are relevant to your students' interests, age, and language proficiency level. For example, if you're teaching grammar to teenagers, you might use song lyrics from popular songs they like.

2. **Set Clear Learning Objectives**: Before using authentic materials, define clear learning objectives related to the grammar point you want to teach. This will help

you focus on specific language structures and ensure that the materials align with your teaching goals.

3. **Adapt Materials as Needed**: Authentic materials may contain complex vocabulary or structures that are beyond your students' current level. Consider adapting or simplifying the materials to make them more accessible while still retaining the grammatical elements you want to teach.

4. **Provide Context**: Give students some background information about the authentic material to help them understand the context in which the language is used. This can include a brief introduction to the topic, the source of the material, or the purpose of the text.

5. **Highlight Target Grammar Structures**: Identify and highlight the specific grammar structures you want to focus on within the authentic material. This can be done through underlining, color-coding, or other visual cues.

6. **Interactive Activities**: Create interactive activities that encourage students to interact with the authentic material. For example, you can design comprehension questions, gap- fill exercises, or sentence transformation tasks that require students to manipulate the target grammar.

7. **Group and Pair Work**: Use authentic materials as a basis for group or pair work. This can involve discussions, debates, or collaborative writing tasks that require students to apply the grammar in a communicative context.

8. **Feedback and Correction**: Provide feedback on students' use of grammar during and after working with authentic materials. Correct any errors and use them as teaching opportunities.

9. **Follow-Up Tasks**: After working with authentic materials, assign follow-up tasks such as writing summaries, creating dialogues, or giving presentations based on the content
they've encountered. This reinforces their understanding of the grammar in a practical context.

10. **Assessment**: Use authentic materials as part of your assessment strategy. You can assess students' grammar skills by having them analyze or manipulate sentences from the materials or by evaluating their performance in follow-up tasks.

11. **Variety of Materials**: Don't limit yourself to one type of authentic material. Use a variety of sources to keep the lessons engaging and expose students to different language styles and registers.

12. **Encourage Critical Thinking**: Encourage students to think critically about the language they encounter in authentic materials. Discuss cultural nuances, idiomatic expressions, and the impact of grammar on the overall meaning of the text.

Using authentic materials in teaching English grammar can make the learning experience more enjoyable and practical for students. It helps bridge the gap between classroom learning and real- life language use, making grammar more relevant and meaningful in their everyday communication.

15-4

Incorporating Technology

Incorporating technology into teaching English grammar can be an effective way to engage students and make learning more interactive and enjoyable. Here are some strategies and tools you can use:

1. Interactive Websites and Apps:
    - There are numerous websites and apps specifically designed to teach English grammar. Platforms like Grammarly, Duolingo, and English Grammar in Use provide interactive lessons and quizzes.
    - Quizlet and Anki are flashcard apps that can help students memorize grammar rules and vocabulary.
    - Grammarly and other proofreading tools can be used to teach students about common grammar mistakes and how to correct them.

2. Online Grammar Games:

- Incorporate online grammar games like Kahoot, Quizizz, or Gimkit into your lessons. These platforms allow you to create fun and competitive quizzes that reinforce grammar concepts.
- Websites like Funbrain and Grammar Ninja offer engaging grammar games for students of all ages.

3. YouTube Videos:
    - There are many educational YouTube channels dedicated to teaching English grammar, such as English with Lucy, Grammarly, and BBC Learning English. These videos can complement your lessons and provide real-life examples.

4. Grammar Blogs and Podcasts:
    - Encourage students to explore grammar blogs and podcasts, such as Grammar Girl's Quick and Dirty Tips for Better Writing. These resources can help students stay updated on grammar rules and usage.

5. Grammar-checking Tools:
    - Teach students how to use grammar-checking tools like Grammarly or Microsoft Word's built-in grammar checker to self-edit their writing assignments.

6. Online Grammar Quizzes and Exercises:

- Websites like Purdue OWL, Grammarly, and the British Council offer a variety of grammar exercises and quizzes that students can access for free.

7. Online Writing Platforms:
    - Platforms like Google Docs and Microsoft Word Online allow students to collaborate on writing assignments and receive real-time feedback on their grammar and writing style.

8. Social Media and Messaging Apps:
    - Encourage students to use social media platforms and messaging apps in English to practice grammar in a real-world context. They can create posts, write comments, and engage in conversations with peers.

9. Virtual Reality (VR) and Augmented Reality (AR):
    - If you have access to VR or AR technology, consider using it to create immersive grammar lessons. Virtual tours, interactive grammar scenarios, and 3D visualizations can make grammar more engaging.

10. Online Grammar Communities:
    - Encourage students to join online grammar forums and communities where they can ask questions, participate in discussions, and share their knowledge with others.

Remember that while technology can enhance grammar instruction, it should complement, not replace, traditional teaching methods. A balanced approach that combines technology with in- person instruction, feedback, and practice is often the most effective way to teach English grammar. Additionally, consider the age and proficiency level of your students when selecting and implementing technology tools in your teaching.

15-5

Assessment and Feedback

Assessment and feedback are crucial components of effective teaching, especially when it comes to teaching English grammar. These processes help students understand their strengths and weaknesses, track their progress, and make improvements. Here are some strategies and tips for assessing and providing feedback in teaching English grammar:

1. Formative and Summative Assessment:
    - **Formative assessment**: This involves ongoing assessments, such as quizzes, homework assignments, and in-class activities, designed to provide feedback during the learning process. It helps identify areas where students may need additional support.
    - **Summative assessment**: These are assessments given at the end of a unit, course, or term to evaluate students' overall understanding of English grammar. Examples include final exams or major projects.

2. Clear Learning Objectives:
    - Clearly define your learning objectives and outcomes for each grammar lesson. This will guide your assessment methods and ensure that your assessments align with your teaching goals.

3. Variety of Assessment Methods:
    - Use a variety of assessment methods to cater to different learning styles and abilities. These can include written tests, oral assessments, presentations, peer reviews, and self-assessments.

4. Rubrics and Criteria:
    - Develop clear and specific rubrics or criteria for assessing grammar assignments. This helps students understand what is expected and provides consistent grading.

5. Timely Feedback:
    - Provide feedback promptly after assessments. Timely feedback allows students to learn from their mistakes and make improvements. Constructive feedback should focus on both errors and strengths.

6. Individual and Group Feedback:

- While individual feedback is essential, consider providing feedback to the whole class as well. This can include going over common mistakes or discussing the overall performance of the class.

7. Peer Assessment:
    - Encourage peer assessment and self-assessment. This helps students develop their critical thinking skills and take ownership of their learning.

8. Technology Tools:
    - Utilize technology tools like grammar-checking software and online platforms that offer immediate feedback on grammar and writing.

9. Portfolio Assessment:
    - Have students maintain a portfolio of their work over time. This can include corrected essays, exercises, and other assignments, demonstrating their progress in English grammar.

10. Adapt to Student Needs:
    - Be flexible in your assessment approach. Adapt to the needs of individual students, providing extra help or challenging assignments as needed.

11. Record Keeping:

- Maintain records of student performance and progress over time. This can help you identify trends and tailor your teaching to address specific challenges.

12. Feedback Sessions:
    - Conduct one-on-one feedback sessions with students to discuss their performance, goals, and areas for improvement. This personalized approach can be highly effective.

13. Celebrate Progress:
    - Acknowledge and celebrate students' progress, no matter how small. Positive reinforcement can motivate students to continue working on their grammar skills.

14. Continuous Improvement:
    - Continuously evaluate your assessment and feedback methods. Ask for feedback from your students to improve your teaching approach.

Remember that effective assessment and feedback are ongoing processes that should be integrated into your teaching practice. By providing constructive feedback and creating a supportive learning environment, you can help your students improve their English grammar skills.

Chapter 16

Resources and Further Reading

Chapter 16-1

Recommended Grammar Books

There are several excellent grammar books available that can help you improve your writing and communication skills. Here are some recommended grammar books:

1. "The Elements of Style" by William Strunk Jr. and E.B. White: This classic book is a concise guide to grammar and style, offering clear and practical advice on writing.

2. "Grammarly Handbook" by Grammarly: This online resource is a comprehensive guide to English grammar and writing, covering a wide range of topics with examples and explanations.

3. "Woe is I" by Patricia T. O'Connor: This book takes a lighthearted approach to grammar and provides clear

explanations of common grammar issues, making it an engaging read for learners of all levels.

4. "Eats, Shoots & Leaves" by Lynne Truss: A humorous and informative book about punctuation, this one is particularly useful if you want to improve your understanding of how to use commas, semicolons, and other punctuation marks.

5. "The Chicago Manual of Style" by The University of Chicago Press Editorial Staff: This is a comprehensive reference manual for writers, editors, and publishers, providing guidelines on grammar, punctuation, and style.

6. "Merriam-Webster's Collegiate Dictionary": A good dictionary is an essential tool for anyone looking to improve their language skills. Merriam-Webster's is a widely respected choice.

7. "The Blue Book of Grammar and Punctuation" by Jane Straus: This book offers clear explanations and examples of grammar and punctuation rules, making it a handy reference for writers.

8. "The Grammar Bible" by Michael Strumpf and Auriel Douglas: This book provides comprehensive coverage of English grammar and usage, with plenty of examples and exercises to reinforce your learning.

9. "Style: Lessons in Clarity and Grace" by Joseph M. Williams and Joseph Bizup: While primarily focused on writing style, this book also covers grammar and offers valuable insights into improving your writing overall.

10. "English Grammar in Use" by Raymond Murphy: This book is an excellent resource for English learners, with clear explanations and a variety of exercises to practice grammar skills.

Remember that different books may suit different learning styles and needs, so it's a good idea to explore a few of these options to find the one that works best for you. Additionally, consider online grammar resources and courses, which can complement your learning from books.

16-2

Online Resources

Teaching English grammar can be made more effective and engaging with the help of various online resources. Here are some online tools and websites that can assist you in teaching English grammar:

1. **Grammarly** (www.grammarly.com): Grammarly is a popular writing assistant that provides real-time grammar and spelling suggestions. While it's primarily used for proofreading, it can also be a valuable teaching tool to explain grammar rules and correct common mistakes.

2. **Purdue OWL** (owl.purdue.edu): The Purdue Online Writing Lab (OWL) is a comprehensive resource for teaching grammar and writing. It offers detailed explanations, examples, and exercises on various grammar topics.

3. **Grammar Bytes!** (www.chompchomp.com): Grammar Bytes! is a fun and interactive website that offers

grammar exercises, handouts, and videos. It's a great resource for both teachers and students.

4. **Grammar Girl** (www.quickanddirtytips.com/grammar-girl): Grammar Girl provides quick and easy-to-understand explanations of common grammar rules. The website also features a podcast that covers various grammar topics.

5. **Cambridge English** (www.cambridge.org): The Cambridge English website provides free resources, including downloadable worksheets, lesson plans, and interactive grammar exercises suitable for learners of all levels.

6. **British Council** (learnenglish.britishcouncil.org/grammar): The British Council offers a wide range of grammar lessons, quizzes, and activities for English language learners. They also have a section specifically designed for teachers.

7. **ESL Tower** (www.esltower.com): ESL Tower provides free grammar games, worksheets, and lesson plans for ESL (English as a Second Language) teachers and students.

8. **BBC Learning English** (www.bbc.co.uk/learningenglish): The BBC Learning English website offers grammar

lessons, quizzes, and videos designed for English learners.

9. **English Club** (www.englishclub.com): English Club offers grammar lessons, quizzes, and interactive activities for learners and teachers. It covers a wide range of topics and levels.

10. **Quill.org** (www.quill.org): Quill is an interactive platform that offers grammar and writing activities suitable for students of all ages. It provides instant feedback and tracks progress.

11. **English Grammar 101** (www.englishgrammar101.com): This website provides free grammar lessons and quizzes covering a wide range of topics. It's suitable for both beginners and advanced learners.

12. **Grammar Monster** (www.grammar-monster.com): Grammar Monster offers grammar rules, examples, and quizzes, making it a helpful resource for learners and teachers.

13. **EngVid** (www.engvid.com): EngVid features a variety of video lessons on English grammar and vocabulary. It's a useful resource for visual learners.

14. **Education.com** (www.education.com): Education.com offers a collection of free grammar worksheets and lesson plans for teachers. It covers various grade levels.

15. **YouTube**: YouTube has numerous channels dedicated to teaching English grammar. Some popular channels include EnglishClass101, Learn English with Rebecca, and Espresso English.

When using online resources for teaching English grammar, it's essential to select materials that align with your students' proficiency levels and learning styles. Additionally, consider blending online resources with in-class activities and discussions for a well-rounded approach to grammar instruction.

16-3

Professional Organizations

There are several professional organizations dedicated to the field of teaching English grammar and language education. These organizations provide resources, support, and networking opportunities for educators, researchers, and professionals in the field of English language teaching and grammar. Here are some prominent ones:

1. **TESOL International Association (Teachers of English to Speakers of Other Languages):**
    - Website: TESOL International Association
    - TESOL is one of the largest and most well-known organizations for English language teaching professionals. It offers a variety of resources, conferences, and publications, including materials related to teaching grammar.

2. **National Council of Teachers of English (NCTE):**
    - Website: NCTE

- NCTE is an organization primarily focused on English language arts education. It provides valuable resources and support for teachers, including those who teach English grammar.

3. American Association for Applied Linguistics (AAAL):
    - Website: AAAL
    - AAAL is an organization dedicated to the scientific study of language. It is a valuable resource for educators and researchers interested in language teaching and grammar.

4. International Association of Teachers of English as a Foreign Language (IATEFL):
    - Website: IATEFL
    - IATEFL is a global organization that focuses on English language teaching and learning. It hosts conferences and offers resources related to grammar instruction and language teaching.

5. Grammar and Writing Organizations:
    - There are also organizations specifically focused on grammar and writing instruction, such as the Grammar and Writing Society (GWS). These organizations may provide specific resources and support for teaching grammar.

6. Local and Regional Organizations: Depending on your location, there may be local or regional associations

or groups of English language teachers who focus on grammar instruction and language education.

7. **Online Communities and Forums:** In addition to formal organizations, there are online communities and forums where English language teachers discuss and share ideas about teaching grammar. Websites like Dave's ESL Cafe, TESL-EJ, and The Internet TESL Journal are examples of such platforms.

When looking to join a professional organization or community related to teaching English grammar, consider your specific interests and needs, as well as whether you want to focus on general English language teaching or a more specialized aspect of grammar instruction. These organizations can provide valuable resources, research, and networking opportunities to enhance your skills as an English language educator.

Chapter 17

Conclusion

17-1

The Ongoing Journey of Grammar Mastery in TESOL

The ongoing journey of grammar mastery in Teaching English to Speakers of Other Languages (TESOL) is a crucial aspect of effective language instruction. TESOL educators continually refine their understanding of grammar and its application to meet the diverse needs of English language learners (ELLs). This journey encompasses various stages and considerations:

1. **Initial Understanding**: TESOL teachers begin their journey by acquiring a solid grasp of English grammar rules and structures. This often involves formal education and training in linguistics, grammar, and syntax.

2. **Pedagogical Strategies**: Educators explore and develop various teaching strategies and techniques to

convey complex grammar concepts to ELLs. This includes using real-life examples, interactive activities, and multimedia resources.

3. **Cultural Sensitivity**: TESOL instructors recognize that language is closely tied to culture. They learn to be culturally sensitive and adapt their teaching methods to ensure that grammar lessons are contextually relevant and respectful of students' backgrounds.

4. **Differentiated Instruction**: Understanding that students have diverse language proficiency levels and learning styles, TESOL educators employ differentiated instruction. They tailor their teaching to cater to the individual needs of each learner.

5. **Continuous Learning**: Grammar rules evolve, and language usage changes over time. TESOL teachers must stay up-to-date with the latest developments in English grammar to provide accurate and relevant instruction.

6. Error Correction: Teachers focus on providing constructive feedback on students' written and spoken language, helping them identify and rectify grammatical errors effectively. They strike a balance between error correction and encouraging fluency.

7. Integration with Other Skills: Grammar instruction is integrated with other language skills, such

as listening, speaking, reading, and writing. TESOL instructors design activities that reinforce grammar concepts in practical communication scenarios.

8. **Authentic Materials**: TESOL educators incorporate authentic materials like newspapers, books, and real-life conversations to expose students to natural language usage. This helps learners grasp grammar in its real-world context.

9. **Professional Development**: Ongoing professional development is a critical aspect of the journey. Teachers attend workshops, conferences, and seminars to exchange ideas, learn new teaching methods, and stay informed about the latest research in language education.

10. **Adapting to Technology**: Technology has transformed language instruction. TESOL educators embrace digital tools and online resources to enhance grammar instruction, making it more engaging and accessible to students.

11. **Assessment and Feedback**: Regular assessment of students' grammar skills is essential. Teachers use assessment tools to gauge progress and provide targeted feedback to help students improve.

12. **Cultural Competence**: TESOL instructors also focus on cultural competence and intercultural

communication. Understanding the cultural nuances of language use is crucial for effective communication.

13. **Lifelong Journey**: Grammar mastery is a lifelong journey for TESOL educators. They continue to refine their skills, adapt to changing language dynamics, and remain passionate about helping ELLs become proficient in English.

In summary, the journey of grammar mastery in TESOL is a dynamic and ongoing process that involves continuous learning, adapting to student needs, and staying current with the ever- evolving world of language education. Effective grammar instruction is not just about rules and structures; it's about empowering students to use English effectively in real-life situations.

Chapter 18

Appendices

- Grammar Exercises and Activities
- Sample Lesson Plans
- Sample Exercises

18-1

Grammar Exercises and Activities

Here are some grammar exercises and activities that you can use to practice various aspects of grammar:

1. **Fill in the Blanks:** Provide a sentence with gaps, and ask students to fill in the blanks with the appropriate words or phrases. This can be used for practicing tenses, prepositions, articles, or vocabulary.
   Example: "I (go) to the store yesterday to buy (apple)."

2. **Error Correction:** Present sentences with grammatical errors, and have students identify and correct the mistakes. This can help improve their proofreading skills.
   Example: "He don't like pizza. → He doesn't like pizza."

3. **Sentence Building:** Give students a list of words or phrases, and ask them to construct grammatically correct sentences or paragraphs using those elements. This can be used to reinforce sentence structure and word order.

Example: Words: "She, dance, every, Saturday." Sentence: "She dances every Saturday."

4. **Verb Tense Timeline:** Create a timeline on the board with past, present, and future markers. Provide sentences, and ask students to place them on the timeline according to the correct verb tense.
   Example: Sentence: "I will visit my grandmother next week." Timeline: [Past][Present] -
   ------- [Future] Placement: "I will visit my grandmother next week." (on the future marker)

5. **Grammar Bingo:** Create Bingo cards with various grammatical elements (e.g., verb tenses, adjectives, adverbs) in the squares. Call out sentences or questions related to those elements, and students mark the corresponding squares on their Bingo cards.

6. **Sentence Transformation:** Provide a sentence and ask students to rewrite it using a different grammatical structure. For instance, change an affirmative sentence to a negative one, or turn a question into a statement.
   Example: Original: "She is studying for the exam." Transformation: "She isn't studying for the exam."

7. **Grammar Scavenger Hunt:** Give students a list of specific grammatical features or rules to find in a text

(e.g., find five present continuous tense verbs). This activity encourages them to analyze real-world language usage.

8. **Grammar Quizzes:** Create quizzes with multiple-choice or fill-in-the-blank questions covering various grammar topics. This is an effective way to assess students' understanding and retention of grammar rules.

9. **Story Writing:** Encourage students to write short stories or paragraphs using specific grammar rules or vocabulary words. This creative activity helps them apply grammar concepts in context.

    Remember to adapt these exercises and activities to the age and proficiency level of your students, and feel free to mix and match them to create engaging and effective grammar lessons.

18-2

Exercise: Reported Speech Practice

Instructions: In this exercise, you will practice converting direct speech into reported speech. Read the following sentences in direct speech and then rewrite them in reported speech. Pay attention to changes in verb tenses, pronouns, and time expressions.

Example: Direct Speech: She said, "I am going to the store." Reported Speech: She said that she was going to the store.

1. Direct Speech: "I will meet you at 3 PM," he said. Reported Speech:
2. Direct Speech: "They have already finished the project," she told me. Reported Speech:
3. Direct Speech: "We are going on vacation next week," they announced. Reported Speech:
4. Direct Speech: "She is cooking dinner tonight," he mentioned. Reported Speech:
5. Direct Speech: "I saw a movie yesterday," she admitted. Reported Speech:
6. Direct Speech: "He has been working here for five years," the manager explained. Reported Speech:

7. Direct Speech: "They are going to have a party on Saturday," Mary said. Reported Speech:
8. Direct Speech: "I have never been to Paris before," he confessed. Reported Speech:
9. Direct Speech: "I am studying for my exams," she informed us. Reported Speech:
10. Direct Speech: "She will call you later," he promised. Reported Speech:

Answers:
1. He said that he would meet me at 3 PM.
2. She told me that they had already finished the project.
3. They announced that they were going on vacation the following week.
4. He mentioned that she was cooking dinner that night.
5. She admitted that she had seen a movie the day before.
6. The manager explained that he had been working there for five years.
7. Mary said that they were going to have a party on Saturday.
8. He confessed that he had never been to Paris before.
9. She informed us that she was studying for her exams.
10. He promised that she would call later.

18-3

Sample Lesson Plan: Conditional Sentence Type Two

Level: Intermediate

Objective: By the end of this lesson, students will be able to understand, identify, and construct conditional sentences of Type 2.

Materials:

- Whiteboard and markers
- Handouts with practice exercises
- Projector and screen (optional)

Duration: 60 minutes

Engagement (15 minutes):

1. **Warm-up:** Begin the lesson with a brief discussion about hypothetical situations. Ask students questions like:

- If you could travel anywhere in the world, where would you go and why?
- What would you do if you won a million dollars? Encourage students to use their imagination and share their answers with the class.

2. **Introduction:** Explain that in English, we use conditional sentences to talk about hypothetical or unreal situations. Today, we'll focus on Conditional Sentences Type 2. Write the following sentence on the board: "If I had more free time, I would learn to play the guitar." Discuss the structure and meaning of this sentence with the class. Emphasize that Type 2 conditionals are used for unreal or unlikely situations in the present or future.

Study (25 minutes):

3. **Grammar Explanation:** Present the structure of Conditional Sentences Type 2:

- **If clause (Condition):** Simple past tense
- **Main clause (Result):** Would + base form of the verb

Write more example sentences on the board, both positive and negative, to illustrate this structure.

1. **Practice:** Distribute handouts with exercises related to Type 2 conditional sentences. Include a mix of fill-in-the-blank, multiple-choice, and sentence transformation exercises. Encourage students to work individually or in pairs to complete the exercises.

2. **Review and Discuss:** Go over the answers to the exercises as a class. Address any questions or uncertainties that arise during the review.

Activation (20 minutes):

6. **Speaking Activity:** Divide the class into pairs or small groups. Provide each group with a set of scenario cards. On each card, there should be a hypothetical situation. Students take turns creating Type 2 conditional sentences based on the scenarios and discussing their hypothetical outcomes.

7. **Group Presentation:** Select a few groups to share their scenarios and sentences with the class. Encourage students to be creative and use the structure correctly.

Conclusion (5 minutes):

8. **Summary:** Recap the key points of the lesson on Conditional Sentences Type 2. Ask students if they have any questions or need further clarification.

9. **Homework:** Assign homework that includes writing a short paragraph or story using at least three Type 2 conditional sentences.

Assessment: Throughout the lesson, observe students' participation in discussions, their ability to complete the exercises accurately, and their use of Conditional Sentences Type 2 in the speaking activity.

By following this lesson plan, students should gain a solid understanding of Conditional Sentences Type 2 and be able to use them in both written and spoken English to talk about hypothetical situations in the present or future.

18-4

Sample Lesson Plan: Present Perfect Tense

Level: Intermediate

Duration: 60 minutes

Objective: By the end of this lesson, students will be able to correctly use and understand the present perfect tense in English.

Materials:

1. Whiteboard and markers
2. Handouts with practice exercises
3. Slides or visual aids (optional)

Engagement (15 minutes):

1. **Warm-up Activity (5 minutes):** Begin the lesson with a quick warm-up activity to engage students' interest in the topic. Write the following sentence on the

board: "I have never been to Paris." Ask students to discuss in pairs or small groups whether they have ever been to Paris or not. Encourage them to use the present perfect tense (have + past participle).

2. **Discussion (5 minutes):** After the warm-up activity, initiate a class discussion about their experiences using the present perfect tense. Ask open-ended questions such as:
    - "Can you share some things you have done in your life that you are proud of?"
    - "Have you ever met a famous person?"
    - "What are some places you have visited recently?"

3. **Lead-In (5 minutes):** Show a picture of a famous landmark or a world map on the board or slides and ask students if they have ever been there. Elicit responses using the present perfect tense.

Study (25 minutes):

4. **Presentation (10 minutes):** Begin the study phase by introducing the present perfect tense. Write the following on the board: "Subject + have/has + past participle." Explain that the present perfect is used to describe actions or events that have a connection to the present. Provide examples on the board, both affirmative and negative sentences:

- "I have visited London." / "I haven't visited London."
- "She has eaten sushi." / "She hasn't eaten sushi."

5. **Guided Practice (10 minutes):** Distribute handouts with practice exercises related to the present perfect tense. Include a mix of fill-in-the-blank, multiple-choice, and transformation exercises. Walk around the classroom to assist students as they work on the exercises.

6. **Review (5 minutes):** Go over the answers to the exercises as a class. Encourage students to ask questions if they have any doubts about the present perfect tense.

Activation (20 minutes):

7. **Role-Play Activity (10 minutes):** Divide the class into pairs or small groups. Provide each group with a scenario card containing a situation where they need to use the present perfect tense. For example, "You are talking to a friend about your life experiences. Use the present perfect to share three things you have done." Allow groups to practice and then have them perform their role-plays in front of the class.

8. **Class Discussion (10 minutes):** Conclude the lesson with a class discussion. Ask students to share what they have learned about the present perfect tense during

the lesson. Encourage them to use the tense in their responses. Also, ask them to reflect on how they can apply this tense in their daily lives.

Homework (Optional): Assign additional exercises or writing tasks related to the present perfect tense for homework to reinforce their understanding.

Assessment: Assess students based on their participation in class discussions, performance in the role-play activity, and completion of the study phase exercises.

Follow-up: In the next lesson, review the present perfect tense briefly, and introduce new tenses or grammar points to continue building students' language skills.

18-5

Sample Lesson Plan: Question Tags

Level: Intermediate to Advanced
Duration: Approximately 90 minutes
Objective: By the end of this lesson, students will be able to correctly use question tags in English sentences, both in positive and negative forms, and understand their usage in different contexts.

ENGAGEMENT (15 MINUTES)

1. Introduction to Question Tags (5 minutes)
    Begin the lesson by introducing the concept of question tags to the students. Explain that question tags are short questions added to the end of a sentence to confirm information or seek agreement. Provide some simple examples:
    - It's a nice day, isn't it?
    - You like coffee, don't you?

2. **Icebreaker Activity: Question Tag Warm-up (10 minutes)**
   Engage the students in a fun activity to get them thinking about question tags. Prepare a list of 5-7 statements and ask students to form question tags for each one. Encourage them to work in pairs or small groups to generate their tags. Afterwards, have each group share their tags with the class.
   Example statements:
   - She's a doctor.
   - We went to the beach last weekend.
   - You've seen that movie before.

   Study (30 minutes)

3. **Explanation of Question Tag Rules (10 minutes)**
   Present the basic rules for forming question tags to the class:
   - For positive statements, use a negative question tag, and vice versa.
   - If the main verb is an auxiliary/modal verb (e.g., is, can, will), use the opposite form in the tag.
   - If there is no auxiliary/modal verb in the main sentence, use "do" (or its variant) in the tag, in the correct form (do/does/did).
   - If the subject is singular, the tag should be singular; if the subject is plural, the tag should be plural.

- If the statement is in the present simple tense, the tag should be in the present simple tense; if the statement is in the past simple tense, the tag should be in the past simple tense.

4. Guided Practice (10 minutes)
   Provide some guided practice exercises on the board or screen for the students to work on together as a class. Make sure to cover different tenses and sentence types (positive and negative). Correct and discuss the answers as a group.
   Examples:
   - She is coming to the party, she?
   - You don't like pizza, you?
   - They have finished their homework, they?
   - He can swim, he?

   –

5. Group Activity: Question Tag Scenarios (10 minutes)
   Divide the class into small groups and give each group a set of scenarios. In these scenarios, students should create sentences with appropriate question tags based on the information provided. Encourage them to use different tenses and sentence types. Afterward, have each group share their scenarios and the accompanying question tags.
   Examples of scenarios:
   - Scenario 1: Your friend just said they have never been to a foreign country.
   - Scenario 2: Your teacher is explaining a new grammar rule.
   - Scenario 3: You and your classmates are discussing a movie you watched last night.

Activation (30 minutes)

6. Role-Play Activity: Using Question Tags in Conversations (15 minutes)
   Have students practice using question tags in conversations. Pair them up and give each pair a set of conversation prompts. They should take turns using question tags in their conversations, keeping in mind the context of the prompts. Afterwards, ask a few pairs to perform their conversations in front of the class.
   Examples of conversation prompts:
   - Talking about weekend plans.
   - Discussing favorite foods.
   - Sharing opinions on a recent news article.

7. Written Exercise: Sentence Completion (15 minutes)

Provide a worksheet with incomplete sentences. Students should complete each sentence with the appropriate question tag. The sentences can cover various topics and tenses. Afterward, check the answers together as a class.

Homework (Optional)

Assign some additional practice exercises or questions for homework to reinforce their understanding of question tags. Encourage students to pay attention to question tags used in real- life conversations and media.

Conclusion (5 minutes)

Summarize the key points of the lesson and remind students to use question tags to engage in more effective communication. Encourage them to practice this grammar point in their daily conversations.

18-6

Glossary

1. **Adjective:** A word that describes or modifies a noun, providing more information about it. For example, in the phrase "red car," "red" is an adjective describing the car.

2. **Adverb:** A word that describes or modifies a verb, adjective, or other adverb, often indicating how, when, where, or to what extent an action is performed. For instance, in the sentence "She sang beautifully," "beautifully" is an adverb describing how she sang.

3. **Conjunction:** A word used to connect words, phrases, clauses, or sentences. Common conjunctions include "and," "but," "or," and "because."

4. **Noun:** A word that represents a person, place, thing, or idea. Examples include "dog," "Paris," "love," and "teacher."

5. **Preposition:** A word that shows the relationship between a noun or pronoun and other words in a sentence. Common prepositions include "in," "on," "under," and "between."

6. **Pronoun:** A word used to replace a noun in order to avoid repetition. Examples of pronouns include "he," "she," "it," "they," and "we."

7. **Subject:** The noun or pronoun that performs the action of a verb in a sentence. It is typically what the sentence is about.

8. **Verb:** A word that expresses an action, occurrence, or state of being. Verbs are the core of a sentence. Examples include "run," "think," "is," and "have."

9. **Tense:** The form of a verb that indicates when an action takes place, such as past, present, or future. English has various tenses, including present simple, past continuous, and future perfect.

10. **Grammar:** The set of rules and principles governing the structure of a language, including its syntax, morphology, and semantics.

11. **Syntax:** The arrangement of words and phrases to create well-formed sentences in a language. It involves the order of words, clauses, and phrases in a sentence.

12. **Morphology:** The study of the structure and formation of words, including prefixes, suffixes, and inflections that change a word's meaning or grammatical category.

13. **Conjugation:** The process of changing the form of a verb to match its subject in terms of person, number, and tense. For example, "I run" and "he runs" demonstrate verb conjugation.

14. **Infinitive:** The base form of a verb, typically preceded by "to" (e.g., "to run," "to eat"). Infinitives are often used as nouns, adjectives, or adverbs.

15. **Clause:** A group of words that contains a subject and a verb and can stand alone as a complete thought (independent clause) or cannot and depends on an independent clause (dependent or subordinate clause).

16. **Phrasal Verb:** A verb combined with one or more particles (typically prepositions or adverbs) that together have a different meaning from the individual words. For example, "give up" means to quit or surrender.

17. **Antecedent:** The noun or pronoun that a pronoun refers to in a sentence. It helps to clarify the meaning of the pronoun.

18. **Direct Object:** A noun or pronoun that receives the action of a transitive verb in a sentence. It answers the question "What?" or "Whom?" after the verb.

19. **Indirect Object:** A noun or pronoun that receives the action of a verb and is typically preceded by the preposition "to" or "for." It answers the question "To whom?" or "For whom?" after the verb.

20. **Parallelism:** The use of similar grammatical structures or patterns in a sentence or paragraph for clarity and rhythm.

21. **Modifiers:** Words, phrases, or clauses that provide additional information about other elements in a sentence. These can be adjectives or adverbs.

22. **Conjugation:** The process of changing the form of a verb to match its subject in terms of person, number, and tense.

23. **Voice:** The grammatical quality that indicates whether the subject of a verb is the doer of the action (active voice) or the receiver of the action (passive voice).

24. **Predicate:** The part of a sentence that contains the verb and provides information about the subject, typically including what the subject does or is.

25. **Article:** A type of determiner that introduces and specifies a noun as either definite (e.g., "the") or indefinite (e.g., "a" or "an").

26. **Predicate Nominative:** A noun or pronoun that follows a linking verb and renames or identifies the subject of the sentence.

27. **Predicate Adjective:** An adjective that follows a linking verb and describes the subject of the sentence.

28. **Subjunctive Mood:** A verb mood used to express hypothetical, unreal, or contrary-to- fact situations, often using phrases like "if I were" or "I wish he were."

29. **Syntax Tree:** A graphical representation of the structure of a sentence, showing how words and phrases are organized according to grammatical rules.

30. **Parallel Structure:** The use of consistent grammatical patterns in a sentence or passage to maintain clarity and balance.